PETO'S PROGRESS

by

Nick Peto

PUBLISHED BY
LONG BARN BOOKS

Ebrington Gloucestershire GL55 6 NW

First Published 2005

Set in Adobe Garamond

Printed and bound in Slovenia.

ISBN 1 902 421 116

PETO'S PROGRESS

by

Nick Peto

LONG BARN BOOKS

For
Three very special ladies
Annie, Lucinda and Zoë

INTRODUCTION

by Dame Diana Rigg

A few months ago, news began to filter out that Nick Peto had written his memoirs. All round the country, jaws began to drop open and whispered enquiries were made. Could this be true? And if so, who might he have mentioned, in the course of telling exactly which story?

My jaw dropped open too, not, I hasten to add because I had anything to fear from Nick's revelations but because the fact that he was able to make the sustained effort required to pen a book seemed a surprising addition to his many talents. Not that he is unlettered – far from it, Nick is very well read. But I couldn't somehow see him as an author

I should have known better.

Nick has always seized the moment, and squeezed every last drop of enjoyment out of it – whether racing, drinking, shooting, fishing, hunting, dining, playing golf and tennis, gambling, flirting and marrying – not to mention practical joking. The prospect of one of his visits must have made many a country-house hostess quake because fire extinguishers do feature quite prominently in the book and the number of wrong turns taken along midnight corridors, the numbers of bedrooms entered 'by mistake' can hardly be counted.

Nick gets away with it all, of course, simply because of his legendary charm.

Mind you, he can claim impressive licence. Shakespeare featured a Peto in *Henry IV Part II* and he, with his best mate Bardolph, became renowned as 'irregular humourists.'

I can discern only one cloud in the sky of our hero's blithely happy world; at his birth, the Good Fairy gave him boundless energy, wit, and charisma – but alas, she forgot to slip a silver spoon into her reticule and subsequently his mouth. As a result, the necessary crust has always had to be earned and though he has sometimes done so by climbing many ladders apparently effortlessly, at others, Nick has slid down many a long, long snake.

His great-grandfather, Sir Morton Peto set the style for his bloodline, as an entrepreneur of imagination – and not a little sexual potency, as the father of fifteen children.

Sir Morton's firm rebuilt the House of Commons in the 1840s, after the fire. He and his partner also built Nelson's column and at this point, time reveals him as Nick's true ancestor, when he thought that, before the revered admiral was plonked on his plinth, it would be a good wheeze to partake of a lunch on top of the column – history does not relate if a table, chairs, glasses, silver, napery, food, wine and the butler were all hauled up there first – but I bet that's how it was.

Friendship is the thread that runs through this book and Nick has a blessed capacity for forming and sustaining it. Old and young, rich and poor, hale or ailing, female and male, he is a steady, thoughtful, affectionate and fun friend to them.

Just don't tell him I said so.

When Nick invited me to write this Foreword to his hilarious book, I asked him what I could say.

'Oh, I don't know – just say, everybody needs a Peto.'

How true.

Diana Lill

CHAPTER 1

BEGINNING

MY MOTHER HAD her steely side. The first thing I remember, vividly, was being pushed in my pram to the bottom of the garden every morning – and left there. Apparently I cried so loudly that Mum felt the further away I was, the calmer the rest of the household would be.

I'm sure I did cry – at being ostracized away from everyone else for hours.

Yet my mother was really very gentle, shy, and loving. Childcare was different then and in fact my first years were incredibly happy.

I was born just after the outbreak of the war, in October 1939. My mother and I, along with my elder sister and brother spent most of the war years in Camberley. My maternal grandfather was the local solicitor, and Camberley was still just a large village, as yet undeveloped. When my Uncle Mic joined his father in the practice – Close and Son – soon after the war, he was quick to see the potential of the surrounding land. He bought as many acres as he could, and eked them out for building over the next twenty-five years.

My father was away for much of the war; he was a regular soldier, so he saw very little of us until the peace of 1945. My mother used to go off every day to work in a factory which made parts for the Spitfires, so we three children were left with Miss Toy, our nanny. Wendy, my sister, was named after a sheep dog which had died on the day she was born. She was three years older than I and Michael was between us.

In 1943, my brother and I were evacuated to Yorkshire, when my mother had to move nearer London to continue working in the munitions factory, which had been relocated. In order to hedge their bets, my parents lodged us in different places. Michael went to Whitby, to a cottage by the sea, (which was blown up a fortnight after he left it – a German bomber returning from a raid, jettisoned its unused bombs as it cleared the English shore, and demolished the little house.) Meanwhile I was sent to the Mill House in Kirkbymoorside, where I was looked after by an elderly lady called Minnie Elliott. My only memory is of the time I was nipped in the bottom by her Pekingese as I tottered across the kitchen floor.

As the war drew to a close, there was much excitement, because we were to move to North Devon where my father was going to stand for parliament in the forthcoming Election – it ran in the family: his grandfather had been an MP, Whig, then Liberal, and his father had represented Barnstaple for twenty-five years, in the Conservative interest, retiring in 1935. My father bought a white turreted house near Bideford, called Kenwith Castle. It wasn't really a castle at all, but a charming looking house dating back to the fifteenth century, with strange battlements along the length of its roof. It was situated a mile from the sea, and on very wild nights one could hear the roar of the mammoth breakers crashing against the cliffs.

I remember the General Election of 1945 well although I was only six. The Germans had signed the instrument of unconditional surrender on the 7th of May, and the Election was to be held on 26th July – so there was not much time to prepare. My dad came back from the war heavily decorated, with a DSO, two Croix de Guerres, a Légion d'Honneur and had been mentioned in despatches five times. I think he was confident of winning the seat, although it had reverted to Liberal during the war years. He went with my mother to his first meeting, which was on the edge of Exmoor. He had made endless notes for his speech and we wished them good luck as they set off in his Humber Super Snipe. When they arrived at the village hall the only person there was the Agent, Major Barnes, who was lighting the gas lights around the little room. Seven-thirty came and went; finally an old couple who lived nearby showed up at about twenty to eight. Since they were diehard Conservatives my father chatted to them for a while and then drove home, his speech still in his pocket.

By the end of the campaign things had livened up greatly. The eve-of-poll rally was at the Corn Exchange in Barnstaple and Major Barnes was to make a short introductory speech. My father was coming on from another meeting, so Barnes had to keep going until he arrived. There were over a thousand people in the building, mainly Conservatives, but also a sprinkling of noisy Liberals trying to disrupt proceedings. Five minutes into the speech a note was passed to the Agent which said 'The candidate's car has broken down – keep talking.' A few minutes later the messenger hurried up to the platform a second time; this message read 'The candidate is on his way; will be with you in ten minutes.' By this stage Major Barnes had completely run out of steam, and the hecklers seemed about to win the day, so he said 'I will now call on Mrs Peto, the wife of our future Member of Parliament, to introduce herself and say a few words.' I was in the front row, and was appalled to hear this announcement. My mother was very shy, and I knew that wild horses would not induce her to make a speech, under any circumstances. Unhesitatingly, I raced up the steps onto the dais – and grabbed the microphone. 'Mummy can't make speeches; she never has, and she never will', I shrilled. There were roars of laughter and applause, and I sheepishly went back to my place. At that moment my father arrived. He won the seat by a very slender majority, at a time when there were only seven Conservative gains in the whole of the 1945 election. I have always maintained that it was my intervention which swung the day.

Michael and I went off each morning to Linfield School in Bideford, while Wendy spent two years at Westbank. We were driven to school each morning by my mother in her Standard Eight. She was a rotten driver (never, of course, having had to take a test). The tiny road we took from Kenwith to the town was called Scratcheyface Lane. It lived up to its name, with high banks on both sides, and huge leaning bramble bushes making an archway above us. You couldn't count the number of small accidents we had. Because of my schooling, I developed a strong North Devon accent, which I still love to hear today. When Major Barnes was awarded the Order of the British Empire, I heard one old boy say to another, '…'e be OBE, 'e be.'

'Oh, be 'e?'

We had bought Kenwith and 300 acres of farmland for just under £2,000. It was a fabulous part of North Devon, dominated by Hubbers Hill to the left of the long drive. This is a steep wood, where a pair of ravens nested in the highest pine tree year after year. Along the valley ran a stream full of trout, with a few sea trout. The banks were very overgrown, and the only way I could winkle out any fish was with a worm on a hook, sitting patiently hour after hour waiting for a bite. I loved to do this, but I became so excited when I finally hooked a fish that invariably I would sling it right over my shoulder. Often it would become detached in flight, only to be lost in the undergrowth behind. It was the interminable time I spent on the bank of this little brook which imbued in me a lifelong love of fishing, and of observing all the wildlife which lived along the river.

My father was keen for us to learn to ride. He had served for thirty years in the Ninth Lancers and was an expert horseman. He was badly wounded at the end of the first World War, and the bullet which hit him remained in his back for the rest of his long life. It was considered too close to his heart to try an operation to remove it. He was shot through his right hand in the Second War, the bullet taking away two fingers and also making a hole in the palm of his hand. Despite these wounds he continued to break in young horses, and to encourage us on our ponies. Things did not always go his way, however. One day I watched him trotting round and round in a circle. The young animal finally became restless, and bolted away down the lane, at the far end of which was our chicken house, so something had to give; at the very last moment the horse stopped, and my papa flew right over the top of the shed – to land on his back in the filthy hen run on the other side. He was a hot tempered man, and I added some new words to my vocabulary that morning.

One of my mother's brothers, Euan, came on a protracted visit. He had been very severely burnt in the war, and his face had undergone some major plastic surgery. He had two little tubes instead of a nose, and his mouth was a small hole in the right cheek. Euan had coped well when he was in hospital, surrounded by other desperately unfortunate men, but, unsurprisingly, he found it impossible to come to terms with all the looks (and sometimes giggles) he evoked when walking down a public street. Every day he was with us, during the autumn of 1946 and regardless of the weather, he would go for a swim in the sea at Westward Ho! He would fight his way through the white breakers as they hurled themselves onto the sand. On Boxing Day he swam off as usual, but this time he did not return to his little bundle of clothes on the beach. He was never seen again.

My parents set about making a really beautiful garden at Kenwith. As anyone who has lived in North Devon will know, the climate is perfect for gardening. No frost in winter; day after day of light rain and low clouds, drooping at the edges like felt. Occasionally there were memorable sunny weeks in the summertime, with blue, blue sky and a sparkling sea. We had a gardener, and a cowman called Jack Hall, whose wife Naomi did our cooking. She was over twenty stone, and a force to be reckoned with when she was in a bad temper. (I never saw her in a good one.)

In the evenings I would listen to countless episodes of Kenneth Horne, in *Much binding in the Marsh.* I also never missed Jock and Snowy's exploits in *Dick Barton – Special Agent*. I spent hours with my Meccano set, trying to build houses and cars.

I joined my brother at his prep school, Cothill House near Abingdon, in the autumn of 1947, just before my eighth birthday. This was a happy establishment, with not too much pressure applied – a school for the average boy. It prided itself on producing lively, happy, appreciative individuals with more virtues than vices. The prefects wore knickerbockers and caps, and were giants in every way to me during my first year. There was inevitably a post-war austerity; many clothing coupons were required to buy the school uniform. Ours was a somewhat spartan regime, and the food was not comparable to what is given to schoolchildren today. I can still remember the revolting taste of waterglass eggs, which was often followed by lumpy junket. We played endlessly with dinkie toys, swopping them, and dragging a whole line of them along on a piece of string. On my first night there I was very homesick. I crept into my bed, a hard friendless little affair with chipped white metal at the head and foot, and covered with two coarse blankets. I remember being about to cry, when the boy next to me was suddenly violently sick onto our communal mat. He was Henry Berens, who shares the same birthday as me, and became a lifelong friend. As I tidied up our mat and chatted to him quietly I felt vastly better – I suppose just knowing that all the new boys were as nervous as me helped a lot.

Most of us listened to the Test matches on the radio during the summer of 1948 – when Donald Bradman and his Australians swept all before them. On Sunday mornings we used to write letters home, which were checked by one of the masters before being mailed. After this, Sundays were ours to do with what we liked until evensong, and then a film show. Some would play golf, some formed themselves into small gangs and roamed the woods and marshes within the grounds. This was a hard afternoon for any boy who was a bit out of the ordinary – too fat, too ugly, too short; they could be teased and bullied at will, as there were no masters around to stop the perpetrators.

My mother would come up from North Devon once a term to take Michael and me out for Sunday lunch. Her mother was one of five sisters, and the other four never married. They lived in a very old-fashioned way on a farm at Brill, near Aylesbury and this was where we always went; we were made enormously welcome by 'The Brill Aunts'. We helped them make butter in the large churn; we would use their splendid knife sharpener: (their knives were thin-bladed, the steel having been sharpened away). We played tennis on their terrible grass court, using balls which were probably pre-war. We helped their farm-hand, Guntrip, with the milking of the three Guernsey cows.

Sundays out at the Manor Farm were idyllic. My great aunts were all huge characters, all religious and all very amusing. Aunty Doffy was the youngest, at about seventy and the fiercest was the oldest, Aunty Olive. When introduced to a new curate who didn't quite catch her name, she repeated it, saying 'Olive. Olive. But I'm not black, I'm not green, and I've never been stuffed.' It was a pre-war set-up, but one of great charm, and many of these old ladies' wise remarks have stayed with me all my life.

One of the masters at Cothill was H A G Phillimore

(known as 'Hag' to all the boys). He seemed to us very, very old and was a great disciplinarian. If one's manners or class work slipped badly, he would throw open the classroom door, shout 'the door is open', and march the offender off to the Headmaster, Sam Pike. Major Pike was a keen advocate of the cane, and used it on us unhesitatingly. He had been a great squash player in his youth, so his wrist was strong and his aim was sure. You did not get beaten a second time if you could help it. But 'Hag' was really a gentle old fellow at heart, and he used to read wonderful books to his class in the dark winter evenings. Fifty years on I can still hear his distinctive, eerie voice, terrifying me with his rendition of *The Hound of the Baskervilles*.

Sam Pike was the epitome of 'firm' but 'fair'. He gave great encouragement to us if we were trying hard, and allowed us to find our own characters and interests. Cothill was where I discovered golf and the little nine-hole course was the cornerstone of my life during my last year. The course was also a place to which one could go with a friend and while away a couple of hours, talking of holiday pursuits – one's prowess with a .410 shotgun, or maybe a description of a day's hunting. Girls were not yet on my radar screen.

There were also four grass tennis courts, not perfect, but adequate. One of the masters, Tom Jackson, taught any boy who expressed interest, and I played every day in the summertime. I loved tennis, and played pretty well by the time I left Cothill. The fees at the school were seventy-five pounds and four shillings a term, and there were a hundred boys. We had cold baths every second morning, before classes started, and always had cold showers after games. Although I was happy there, and lucky to have an elder brother to guide me in my first couple of terms, it was a tough life, both in and out of class. I remember a master called Leonard Swinbank, a cruel, didactic man, throwing a wooden-backed duster at me and hitting the side of my head – no doubt I deserved it, but I did have to be stitched up. In 1949 we had an outbreak of poliomyelitis, at the same time as a 'flu epidemic, which made those with 'flu extremely alarmed in case they too had polio. One boy died, but the three others who had contracted this dreadful disease eventually recovered completely. Michael Abel Smith, Henry Lopes, Seton Wills, Henry Berens and I were given our cricket colours on the same day. We are still all good friends. How lucky our generation has been to have escaped the privations and wars that cut such a swathe through England in the previous fifty years.

By 1952 my sister was already growing into the beautiful girl she later became. She had dark shining hair and very long legs. At this point, aged sixteen, she was still only thinking of her pony, and her hunting with our local pack, the Torrington Farmers. She kept two ferrets in a cage by the dog kennels. One of these, Freddie, was very tame, and Wendy invariably used to have him with her. A French girl, Chantal, came to stay with us for a month that summer to learn English; she put her face too close to the ferret's nose for his liking, and he bit her on the bottom lip. She went to the hospital – ferret still attached – and Freddie had to be sedated before his sharp yellow teeth could be prised open. Chantal left for home the next morning, poor girl – still in tears, and somewhat disfigured.

Wendy's first indoctrination to the attentions of an admirer came in a car on our way to swim in the sea at Westward Ho! We had the Morley family staying and the elder son, David, was a wild but very attractive fellow. We set off for the beach with my father driving, and my brother Mike and I in the front with him. David had hopped into the back with my sister and her dog. We were already in our swimming things, since changing on that vast tract of sand at Westward Ho! wasn't easy, especially if there was a high wind. My father was about to take the right turn down to the beach, when he looked in his mirror to check if there was a car behind. All he saw was David's hand cupped round one of his beloved daughter's breasts. He had scooped it out of her bathing dress, and had it in his hand as if it was a valuable piece of Meissen china. Wendy looked calm and happy, but at that moment the brakes were jammed on hard and we all shot forward in the car. David was told in no uncertain terms to put the breast back where he had found it, and that it was time for him to go for a long swim in the cold sea water.

One of our neighbours lived on the river Torridge at Beam and the three of us used to go over and picnic near the Golden Pool while the grown-ups fished for salmon. Janie Martin, the daughter, was my brother's age – but I was the one who adored her. I followed her slavishly wherever she went and longed for a kind word or a touch from her. My love was not reciprocated, and I later discovered that she fancied my brother a lot, (having been seen by Wendy giving him a kiss while they sat on their ponies out hunting.) At the time I knew only of my love for her, and I dreamt of her at night – the most useless dreams, really, because I had no idea what I hoped from her – I just felt I wanted to be close to her, but beyond that was a fog of exciting uncertainty.

Our holidays at Kenwith developed into a pattern. In the summer we went to the beach almost every day, rain or shine. On the good days we invariably went to Westward Ho! one of the great beaches in the south-west, nearly two miles long; when the tide is out, there is a mile of sand between the sea and the famous pebble ridge, a pile of smooth, sea-washed stones, about twenty or thirty feet high that runs the entire length of the beach. It is a barrier which has evolved naturally over the centuries, and prevents the land behind from being flooded. When the weather was poor, we would explore one of the other shores – Abbotsham Cliffs were steep and awesome, giving way to miles of rocky pools. The sea would cover these at high tide, but as it went out we used to catch prawns by the dozen under the slippery seaweed. We would run from pool to pool in our gym shoes wielding prawning nets, with bags slung over our shoulders. Prawning was a great art, and one had to turn a blind eye to the other inhabitants of the deep clear pools – masses of crabs, the occasional conger eel and sometimes a flatfish darting from under one's feet.

In the winter holidays we rode our ponies, hunting whenever possible over the Devon grasslands. The obstacles were similar to those in Southern Ireland – banks, trappy streams and bogs to scramble through. Michael and I learnt to shoot, but there was little to shoot at, except rabbits and a few pigeons. At dusk one August evening I shot a bird which I mistook for a pigeon. I picked it up, and sadly realising my mistake, I took it home to look it up in my bird book. I identified it as a Greek hawk, which had last been seen in England in the 1850s. I wrapped it up in a box as carefully as I could and sent it off the next morning to the Natural History Museum for verification. It was about three weeks later in that hot summer that I received a one-liner back from the museum 'Dear Sir, With reference to the common cuckoo you sent us in an advanced state of decay...'

I liked nothing better than to wander down the hedgerows trying to shoot a rabbit. Sometimes I would build a rudimentary hide, and would sit behind it for several hours waiting for a pigeon or two to be attracted by my decoys in the stubble behind me. These are the ways to learn field craft: there is nothing like trial and error to hone ones skill. I shot my first pheasant in 1952 at Castle Hill, now a famous shoot, where high pheasants pour over, like pins up in the sky.

It was a quiet and pleasant life. But on the night of August 15–16, 1952 something happened to change that peaceful area of Devon. The Lynmouth flood disaster was the worst, most tragic catastrophe ever to hit the West country. An astounding nine inches of rain fell on Exmoor in 24 hours – most of this deluge occurring between seven in the evening and midnight. It had been raining hard for the previous fortnight, and this final downpour proved too much for the already sodden peat bogs to absorb. There was nowhere else for the water to go, but down the valleys of the East and West Lyn.

An estimated 3,000 million gallons of muddy water and uprooted trees hurtled down the steep slopes towards the seaside village of Lynmouth. Occasionally the rubble and boulders would be held up for a while by one of the bridges and this produced a dam-like effect, until the sheer weight carried the bridge away, and a wall of water careered towards the next barrier. It was these violent surges which were responsible for the appalling damage in the village itself. Thirty four people were drowned in the indescribable mayhem. Huge fifteen-ton boulders were strewn about what used to be streets. Entire houses, hotels, and guesthouses were washed away without trace.

My father, being the local MP, was alerted in the early hours, and he drove over at first light to see the broken village. Wendy and I went with him, and I can still visualise the incredible carnage that lay before us, as we crested the hill. Some houses had been cut in two by the wall of water and debris. Beds and furniture dangled precariously; cars floated in the sea; there were fire engines, police cars and ambulances. A vast chocolate stain extended in a semi-circle half a mile out, denoting the perimeter of the muddy water's progress into the sea.

Of course, this was the peak holiday season, and the resident population of Lynmouth had increased from four hundred and fifty to twelve hundred. By nine o'clock on the evening of the fifteenth, the hydro-electric plant which powered the village had been flooded, and all electricity had ceased. By now it was pitch dark, and the deafening roar of the storm and the angry torrent as it hurtled down its deadly path must have been terrifying. A row of ten cottages which were nearest the moorland was washed away completely. The only evidence of them that we could see the following morning was a sign that swung in a tree advertising 'Bed and Breakfast'.

Twenty-eight bridges were swept away that night. It was

reckoned that over 1,000,000 tons of boulders had rumbled into the village. Eighteen boats were lost, and one hundred and twenty motor cars had been carried out to sea. The horrors of that flood will still be fresh in every survivor's mind. I didn't get there until it was all over, but the devastation of Biblical proportions is as vivid a memory for me now as if it had happened yesterday, and seems to have drawn a line under my happy early childhood.

CHAPTER 2

TAKING TEA WITH NATALIE WOOD

IN THE AUTUMN of 1952, I joined my brother Michael at Eton. After two five-hour journeys to London, to visit Tom Brown the tailors, I was correctly kitted out with tail-coats and masses of other new clothes until I was finally ready. The new boys' tea-party, where doting parents said goodbye to their red-eyed sons, was a most wretched affair. There were six new boys going to the same house as me, D G Bousfield's, and we stood around not knowing where to put ourselves, or what to say. Donald Bousfield was a tremendous housemaster, and had been through this saga many times before. No sooner had our parents departed, than we were each taken by a slightly older boy and shown to our rooms, and it was extremely exciting to have one's own, although in 1952 they were still very basic. There was a little desk, and an ottoman for games clothes. By day my bed was upright against the wall to make more floor space and I had to lower it each evening just before bedtime. The room had a very small fireplace, and each of us had a supply of coal, enough to make a fire about twice a week. In the winter, we took it in turns to congregate in whoever's room had a fire that evening. There was no central heating, so the cold was indescribable in those rooms which were fire-less, but we did not seem to mind.

There were good houses and poor houses, largely depending on the housemaster in question. D G Bousfield was outstanding – a Wykhamist, a superb athlete, and the best communicator with boys imaginable, so his house was a lucky choice for me, and I had five wonderful years at Eton, largely as a result of the encouragement and kindness of this splendid man. Four of the other new boys who arrived with me have remained lifelong friends – people say that one's best friends are made at school, and this is certainly true in my case. The practice was to have high tea with two or three contemporaries and one could only change round at the beginning of each term. My first mess-mates were Derek Strauss, Henry Keswick and Edward Lane Fox. Later, Henry moved to other pals, and we were joined by his brother, Chips Keswick. Chips, Henry, Derek and Edward have been great allies throughout my life, steady and loyal always and brimming with common sense. We have shared endless dramas, but lots of laughter and happiness as well.

In those early days the Dame (matron) kept a close eye on the new entry of boys and she was virtually the only female we came across during the entire time we were at Eton; she made sure we were not unhappy, and administered to the sick – though illness was not acceptable, one simply didn't get ill – it was considered very poor form.

Was there sex at Eton? Well, there was a backdrop of adolescent eroticism, but actual homosexuality never crossed my horizon. Boys had crushes on one another from time to time and there were probably unnaturally close friendships, but I believe anything more than this was extremely rare; certainly in DGB's I would say that it very seldom happened. I do remember going to bed one evening during my first term, and finding a note on my pillow. It read, 'Can I come and see you? If you don't like the idea, please leave a note on top of the lavatory cistern next door.' I didn't know what the fellow was on about and I knew that I didn't want him to visit me, but I thought that I'd leave a note saying 'No, thank you' the next morning. There seemed to me to be no hurry to get out of my warm bed and do it immediately. How wrong I was. Hardly had I gone to sleep, when I was woken by someone opening my door. I screamed like a stuck pig, and the brute fled. Who he was, and exactly what he was after I have never been sure.

For the next two or three years I was also completely unaware of the opposite sex. I had realised my heterosexuality for the first time with the delectable Janie Martin, but when my ardour was not reciprocated, I think I must have forgotten all about it for a few years. There were certainly boys who were far more advanced than me. Martin Summers, (still a good friend and now married to my first wife) was a pretty active fellow. He finally had to leave a week or two before the end of his last term, as he was caught in bed with a very pretty Swedish boys' maid – with whom he had liaised for six months. Another friend of mine was sacked for a similar misdemeanour. What a strange attitude the school had; I don't believe one would have been sent down if one had been caught in bed with a boy.

In my last year, like most of the other seniors, I had a 'fag', a term for a junior boy who had to look after a senior in his final year, to tidy his fag-master's room, cook his high teas, and generally make sure that his life ran smoothly. I used to insist that my 'fag' turned on the shower for me after I had played games, and he had to be standing under it, with soap at the ready, when I arrived, to ensure it was exactly the correct temperature.

While DGB was my housemaster, my classics tutor was David Macindoe, an erudite and charming man who managed to make one really look forward to his classes. 'Early school' still existed, quite a test for both pupils and masters alike. We boys were woken at quarter to seven, and after a quick wash (plus tea and biscuits for those up in time), the first lesson began at 7.30. If the master was fifteen minutes late, the class was allowed a 'run', which meant the boys all ran back to their houses and were allowed to skip that lesson – it did happen, but not very often.

One of the reasons that Eton has remained a top public school is that individuality is very actively encouraged. There is masses of free time, during which it is hoped that boys will pursue whatever really interests them. They can read books, play sport or a musical instrument, paint, act – everything is there, and the preference of each boy is catered for. For this reason, Eton has produced a wide variety of famous old boys; prime ministers and poets, soldiers and statesmen, artists and actors. I was an average student, good enough to coast along without fear of failing exams, and so I was able to concentrate on sport. I took up the game of Rackets during my first term and my father was appalled that my bill for Rackets lessons – and for broken rackets – was over a hundred pounds, while my school fees were only slightly more, at £140. Rackets is a wonderful game, like a very fast version of squash, played on a court three times as large and with a hard ball. I played the team games, cricket and the Field Game (a mix between rugby and soccer), as well as Fives and tennis, and was captain of the squash team for two years.

I had a friend, Tom Troubridge, with whom I used to go on shooting expeditions to the Slough sewage farm. This is a longish walk from school, so we couldn't go often, and of course it was out of bounds to us anyway. We had fold-up .410s which we hid in our tail-coats. I shot my first snipe on that sewage farm. To this very day, if I drive down the M4 with a south wind blowing I still think of those adventures, as the stench of the sewage wafts its way into my car.

When there was a cold snap in the winter, we used to be taken skating on a lake in Windsor Great Park – always a most exciting outing, since the girls from Heathfield used the same venue. As soon as our bus was spotted by the Heathfield mistresses, they used to herd their girls as fast as possible to the far end of the ice, with us Etonians in hot pursuit.

It was at about this time that many of us received an invitation to a Students Ball at Claridges. We had to send £5 to the organiser for a double ticket. He was called Duncan Davidson, and his address was Ampleforth College, in Yorkshire. Many of us sent off for tickets, but nothing ever came back. There was no Ball, and Duncan made a tidy sum. Years later, he went on to found a housebuilding company which eventually became the biggest in Great Britain. He amassed a large fortune and bought more land than any other British individual in the last quarter of the twentieth century. He had a shaky start with his idea of a fictitious dance, but from there he went from strength to strength. He has always been a most generous philanthropic man, a wonderful father to his four girls, and a very good friend to me.

I only once got into any serious trouble at Eton. I was a very poor artist, but we all had to do one hour's art class each week with one of the masters. I was taught by Wilfred Blunt, (brother of Anthony Blunt, later convicted for being the 'fifth man' in the Russian spy scandal with Burgess and Maclean.) On this particular occasion we were each told to draw an Inn sign which we had to imagine would be hung on the outside of a pub. St Andrew's Day, which is always the last Saturday in November, was a whole holiday, when our parents came to visit us, watch us play games, and see what we had done in the previous weeks. Our Inn signs were to be exhibited in the art school for everybody to look at. Mr Blunt knew that I was a very poor student: I was always at the back of the class and he seldom came to look at my efforts. However, just before St Andrew's Day arrived he examined my three foot by four foot work, and asked me what it was. I told him it was the 'Cock and Pullet'. He looked a bit closer and realised that it was extremely obscene. I was bundled off to the headmaster with the offending picture under my arm. When I arrived at Mr Robert Birley's office I was told to put the painting against the wall, while the great man stood back and had a good look at it. Luckily for me, however, he was a brilliant academic and his mind was a very long way from my adolescent thoughts, so he did not recognise my painting as anything wicked; he said he couldn't understand what all the fuss was about.

I was a Sergeant in the Corps, which was a mixed blessing. I once had to take a group on a night map-reading exercise on

Dartmoor which ended in an almighty muddle. Amongst the platoon were two close friends, Chips Keswick and Henry Lopes, neither of whom could have been less interested in the Army and who had arrived at the start point with every intention of making my life difficult. They had somehow procured a bottle of whisky, on which they proceeded to get very tight, and all my cajoling and entreaties to make them move were in vain. Chips, Henry and one or two others just sat on a wall giggling and telling me to push on, and that they would follow shortly.

The following morning, when I arrived at the finish with only three of my five soldiers I was given a severe rocket by the officer in charge. I told him there was very little I could do about Keswick and Lopes, and, when they were eventually located, Chips was sacked from the Corps, much to his delight. I suggested that Roo d'Erlanger should be made up to Lance Corporal, because he had been so helpful; the officer agreed, but when this proposition was put to d'Erlanger he politely refused, on the grounds that the responsibility that went with a single stripe was far too great for him.

By the time my last Eton term came round I was lucky enough to have been made a member of Pop – which is like being a prefect. My contemporaries and I had all gained in confidence and thought we were far greater fellows than we were. In the previous holidays I had been to see the film *Rebel Without a Cause*, starring Natalie Wood. In typical adolescent fashion, I simply could not get this incredible girl out of my mind – or my dreams. She was nineteen years old and already a Hollywood icon, with over fifty films under her belt. She was still unmarried and not only was she a great beauty but she simply overflowed with sex appeal.

Then one day, I read in the paper that she was in London to shoot a new film. What the hell, I thought, I'm damn well going to try and get in touch with her. So I sat down and wrote a short letter to Natalie, asking her to come down to Eton the following Sunday and have tea with me at The Cockpit, on Eton High Street, a spot famous for its wonderful cream teas. I said that afterwards we could go to Evensong in College Chapel.

I found out the name of the hotel where she usually stayed in London and sent the letter off. Then came the anxious wait for a reply. In my heart of hearts I really didn't expect to get one, of course, but I still prayed hard. Two days later, I got a note, saying she would love to come down to Eton.

My emotions were in turmoil with excitement at the prospect of meeting this fantastic girl fighting with trepidation that she either might not turn up after all or, if she did, would find me wanting. At the last minute, I got cold feet, and persuaded David Morley to make up a threesome.

Natalie arrived, chauffeur-driven, and looking even more amazing in the flesh than I had imagined possible. On top of that, she was totally charming, and very tactile. I was in heaven at my tea party.

Afterwards, the three of us walked up the aisle of College Chapel, the envy of every single person there. What an incredible afternoon!

College Chapel was a wonderful building in which to worship. The singing, by the choir of about sixty boys, was truly remarkable. I think everybody who was lucky enough to go there for three or four services a week during their time at Eton must have many happy memories. I remember the Reverend Tomkins telling us from the pulpit that his sermon was going to be on 'constipation.' He took as his text 'and The Lord took two tablets and went up into the hills.' Anything to get our undivided attention.

Another parson who took services regularly was the Reverend Wild. He used to be known to us boys as Rubberneck Wild. The poor fellow had been gassed in the war and his neck stuck out at a strange angle, which caused merriment amongst his pupils. One day he reminded us that once a term if we took Communion on a Wednesday afternoon we were allowed to skip the two last lessons that day. He said that this service was poorly attended, and he hoped very much to see more of us there in the weeks to come. Word went round that we were all to turn up the following Wednesday to this service. About 200 of us went to College Chapel that afternoon. Rubberneck looked around in amazement on entering the church and immediately went off and consecrated several bottles of communion wine. He came back and took the service. But just at the time we were meant to go up to the rail to take communion, we all filed quietly out. The Church of England rule is that once the wine has been consecrated, the celibrant must drink whatever is left over. So we waited outside, and sure enough a little while later the poor Reverend Wild staggered out, having done his very best to drink all the bottles he had prepared for us. How vile can young boys be? Rubberneck Wild was in fact a charming man, who had been extremely brave in the war.

My French master was Mr Seymour – nicknamed Sod. He

had lost a lung at Alamein, and spoke with a very clipped accent. When it was time to do our French précis, he would say 'Pliez le papier pour faire une marge, et mettez la date, et votre nom' in this extraordinary voice. One day I was in the chemist shop, and Sod Seymour was in front of me in the queue. He said to the girl 'Can I have sum pepper, plis?' The girl said 'I'm sorry we don't sell pepper.' 'Don't be frivolous, toilet pepper is what I want.'

Mr Mayes also tried to teach me French. He was known as 'Toady', since he was 90% blind and very small and round. Occasionally we used to hang an overcoat on the back of the door just before he arrived. We all stood up when he entered the room. 'Sit down' Toady would say. So we sat down. Then he would blink behind his pebble spectacles. 'Sit down, I said.' 'We are sitting down, Sir.' 'Well, what's that fool at the back still standing up for then?' he would bellow – pointing at the overcoat.

My brother was captain of his House and his Housemaster was a large fellow called Bud Hill. Two very wayward boys in that house were Michael Barclay and Michael Allhusen, and after one particularly hair-raising escapade they knew that a note had been sent to Bud Hill, explaining what they had done and demanding that they be severely punished.

The two Michaels crept into their Housemaster's study at nine o'clock that evening and started rummaging around, desperately trying to find the note and run off with it.

Suddenly they heard heavy footsteps coming up the stairs, so they ducked quickly behind the curtains. Bud Hill entered and sat down behind his desk. He shuffled papers back and forth, humming quietly to himself. After two whole hours, he said in his deep voice, 'I don't know about you two, but I'm off to bed.'

In 1955 my father retired from being a Member of Parliament, sold Kenwith, and bought a lovely Queen Anne house, Lockeridge House, near Marlborough. Built of red brick, with large, welcoming pomegranates on the gate pillars, Lockeridge had eight bedrooms and eighty acres of land. The upper reaches of the river Kennet ran through our fields, and right past the front of the house. There were two cottages with the property, and the total cost to my father was £14,000.

As a family we didn't really do 'abroad'. The only holiday that we went on en famille was in 1954 to Obergürgl. The skiing was very basic – as yet there were no ski lifts, so one went back up the mountain with the aid of 'skins', which had to be secured under the skis at the end of each run. My father hated the holiday, and couldn't get the hang of skiing at all. His temper, often near the surface, was in complete charge by the end. We were all thankful to get home, to the routine and to the animals, which presented no challenge.

I did go to Venice with my parents, several years later – it rained incessantly for the three days we were there, but a truly remarkable thing happened when we went to the casino. Although my mother disapproved of gambling, she was given the equivalent of a few pounds to keep her quiet while my father played chemin de fer. My mum and I went to the roulette table, where she put her chips on number nine, her lucky number. Number nine duly turned up, and we both rushed off to tell my father that she had made thirty-five times her money. 'Excellent,' he said, 'Where are the chips?' In the excitement, my mother had sped off before raking them in. She raced back to the table, but the next spin of the wheel was already in motion. '*Rien ne va plus,*' called the croupier as we arrived. All my mother's winnings were still on number nine. Nothing to be done, but watch the little ball bouncing round and round the wheel. Eventually it slowed, and then came to a halt – on nine again! The three pounds originally staked, no more than ten minutes previously, had mushroomed into £3500. We had a totally free holiday, and loads of cash as well.

CHAPTER 3

LOVE FOR SALE...

I WAS DESTINED for a career in the army, so I was not able to take any time off between Eton and going to Sandhurst. There was to be no gap year for me. The first six weeks at the Royal Military Academy were very tough. We had a fearsome Sergeant-Major, 'Peanuts' Graham, of the Scots Guards in charge of Inkerman Company, in Old College. I was terrified of him; he used to scream 'I call you Sir, and you call me Sir – the only difference is that you mean it and I don't.' But as the year rolled on, I realised that most things he said were tongue in cheek. His aim, I think was to reduce cadets to their lowest possible ebb, thereby knocking the stuffing out of conceited public schoolboys – and then, after a couple of months, to try and build us up again into a mould which would stand us in good stead as young officers in the army.

There was not much academic work done until later in the curriculum. The first three months were spent on the parade-ground 'square-bashing', and in rigorous sport – long cross-country marches, fearsome obstacle courses, and the thing I most dreaded, the 'junior' cadets boxing tournament. This competition was prehistoric, because names were simply drawn out of a hat, regardless of weight or height. The fellow I was to meet in my first bout was a vast, six foot four inch

Ghanaian, weighing 16 stone. My pal Patrick Anson was a brilliant, fearless boxer and he gave me some helpful tips. However, the day before my début in the ring, I vaulted longways over the wooden horse in the gym and somehow broke my left wrist. I have never been so pleased with an injury. At the end of the competition Inkerman Company had won the cup; everyone felt so sorry for my having been unable to take part, that they asked me to sit in the middle of the team photograph. I still feel a complete fraud when I look at that picture, with me holding the enormous trophy.

My time at Sandhurst became more and more fun as the pressure and work were relaxed. We played many pranks – one of the more successful of which was diverting all the early morning traffic off the A30, which ran in front of the Military Academy's main gate, and onto the parade ground, by means of a series of road signs we had found in an old shed. Once on the parade ground there was nowhere for the traffic to go, and by the time we arrived for our drill parade at 8am there was pandemonium, with lorries, buses and cars full of furious drivers and passengers.

On Guy Fawkes' evening, Old College was set upon by the cadets from New College. The whole episode rapidly grew violent, and as I raced up some steps I saw a fellow hurl a bucket of something towards me. I turned my back – and it was as well I did so, because the bucket was full of boiling water. I screamed, ran straight into a wall and passed out. Some cadets gathered round and, meaning well, pulled off my T-shirt. In so doing they removed all the skin from my back. I spent the next six weeks in hospital face down while it began to re-grow – a very unpleasant experience, not least because it is almost impossible to go to the loo when lying on one's front. I had a large D-shaped wire contraption over my body so that no bed clothes could touch me. Sometime later the guy who threw the water came to apologise. I said that I hoped I would never see him again. Strangely, he went into the 12th Lancers, and I was commissioned into the 9th. A year after we left Sandhurst these two Regiments amalgamated into the 9th/12th Lancers, so Hew Kennedy and I had to spend the next six years in the same Officers Mess.

I became friends with a young man from Thailand called Somchai Danargaata. He was very keen to do well, but for some reason often overslept, so one morning just before he was due on parade, I woke him up and helped him into his kit. That evening he presented me with a beautiful gold Rolex watch to thank me. I decided to make sure I had him on parade every morning, on time and looking smart, to see what else came my way. Sadly, that was it – but I still have the watch, forty-five years later.

There was a parachuting club at Sandhurst which I thought it would be a good idea to join. I discussed the possibility of applying with my pal Andrew Parker Bowles. We both thought that, actually, we wouldn't much enjoy parachuting, but would sign up anyway, so that the powers-that-be would mark us down as enthusiastic potential officers. As only twelve people were ever selected out of two hundred eligible, naturally we did not expect to be among them. Needless to say, we were both chosen. We headed off to Abingdon for our first jump, after spending a couple of days training in the gym learning how to do a parachute roll, and how to exit the aeroplane without getting tangled up. There was a very unpleasant corporal from the Parachute Regiment in charge of us and he took an instant dislike to me. (It is possible that I was cheeky.) On the second morning we were going through our paces in the gym and he said to me 'Mr Peto, sir, I'll get you, you little sod. Don't you worry about that.'

The following day we were to be sent up, in fours, in a small box underneath a barrage balloon which was on a wire attached to the ground. The corporal, three other cadets and I went up, the helium balloon rising steadily. Every hundred feet a flag came out on the wire. After about 300 feet the fellows left on the ground looked very small indeed, like a circle of sheep, and I would like to have taken my chance and jumped out at that point. However, in order for a parachute to open properly, one must be at least 900 feet up. When we got to the required height the corporal slipped back the trap door in the floor of our cubicle. 'Mr Peto, you first,' he shouted, 'stand to the door – GO!' I trickled out of the hole, and a fraction after I had left the box, the corporal screamed down at me 'Come back! come back! come back!' 'Shit, I'm a dead man,' I thought. I desperately tried to climb back – but of course I couldn't, I was on my way. Had he forgotten to hook me up to the static wire in the box? After about five seconds (which seemed like an eternity) my parachute billowed open, and I sailed gently to the ground, cursing the corporal. He had said he would get his own back on me; I really thought I was done for.

The training and drill during the two-year course was extremely thorough. Many of the military instructions which were banged into my head will always remain with me. 'When crawling towards an enemy position remember 'shape, shadow, silhouette, surface, spacing, movement'; 'dash, down, observe, crawl, sights, fire'. I still use military headings when trying to solve a problem: 'Situation, Mission, Execution, Logistics, Command and Signals. Any questions?' We had masses of TEWTS (Tactical Exercise Without Troops) in the classroom. These were extremely effective, and the cloth model had great verisimilitude. One could take a whole day working on the correct tactical approach to defeat the enemy.

It was during my last term at Sandhurst that my friend Charlie Hornby asked me one afternoon whether I had ever slept with a girl. When I told him I had not, he said it was high time this was rectified; we would set off for London that evening to do the deed. His parents had a very grand flat in Montagu Square, just north of Marble Arch. Charlie picked me up in his wooden-backed Morris Minor van, and we headed off for London in a high state of excitement.

We decided our first trawl should be Hyde Park, so we drove slowly along in the hope of seeing an attractive looking prostitute. After a few minutes we spotted a very smart young girl standing on a corner, and so Charlie stopped the car. He leaned across me in the front seat and asked her how much she would charge. Her answer was £5, so he told her to climb in the back. He then asked her whether she had a friend who would come with us; she said she certainly had, and the friend was summoned from the darkness of a nearby tree. A vast girl appeared and tried to get into the front seat with me – so I hopped over into the back. I couldn't imagine doing anything with this lady, but Charlie seemed to think that everything was fine, and so we set off for Montagu Square.

We had already made certain preparations in the flat for our return, which included running a hot bath, because we were terrified of catching some disease. The idea was to jump straight into the bath after any action had taken place. In the hall we spun a coin to decide who should go up to the bedroom first. I won the toss, and told my enormous friend to go on up. I watched her waddling up, step by step, bottom swinging, and I became extremely excited. Unfortunately, I was unable to control myself, and everything happened in my trousers on the way up the stairs. The lady lay down on Charlie's mother's linen sheets and rolled her polo neck up over her bosoms, so that it was more or less around her neck. I asked if she would mind taking it off completely, but she said that would be an extra £3. I said OK – so off came the jersey, without damaging the large beehive hairdo (which was covered in hundreds and thousands). I took my trousers and underpants off and proceeded to make a tremendous show of making love. After a while I said, 'Phew, that was fantastic.' Obviously, because I had been untidy on the staircase, I was unable to do anything at all on top of the lady. Nevertheless, I shot downstairs and jumped into the bath, as if everything had proceeded normally on the bed. My new friend sashayed down the stairs, and I heard her say to Charlie, 'Does he do this often then?' to which Charlie replied, 'Good Lord yes, he's really quite a stud.'

'You could have fooled me,' she said.

Anyway, half an hour later and £8 poorer a-piece, we drove the ladies of the night back to their tree in Hyde Park – me still with my virginity intact.

It may surprise you to learn that I managed to pass out of Sandhurst 3rd top cadet, and in so doing I won the Cavalry Sword. This was possibly the pinnacle of my life – a classic case of peaking too soon.

In July 1959, I was asked out of the blue to spend a weekend at Blenheim. Charles Spencer-Churchill, an old friend from Eton, had invited me, and was the reason I had many, many happy visits to his parents' home. I love Charles: he is a life enhancer par excellence. If the ultimate justification for living is to bring happiness to others, then Charles has certainly had a worthwhile life. Whenever I meet him, I always feel better for the encounter. So, with a sense of anticipation, I set off from Sandhurst in my open Triumph One, a two-seater sports car with huge headlights, and bucket seats in the boot for passengers. I entered Woodstock, and swung in through the enormous wrought iron gates. There was quite a crowd milling about, and on seeing me they all started cheering. I was surprised, but never having been to a Palace before, I thought maybe this was the norm. The hood of the car was down on this beautiful summer day, so I took my cap off and started waving back. I felt like Toad of Toad Hall.

There was a smattering of people all the way up the long drive, and they waved and cheered me as I went by. This is the life, I thought. Eventually, I drew up alongside the vast steps going up to the Palace, and I was about to hop out, when a lady leaned over the passenger door. She said, 'I am the Duchess of Marlborough, you must be Nick Peto.' 'Indeed I am,' I said. I was about to thank her for coming out to meet me, when she said, 'Well, will you pull your car on a bit, as

Sir Winston is right behind you.' Of course, I had not looked in my mirror the whole way up the drive, and now I felt very small indeed. Churchill got out of his car, and he put his arm round my shoulder as we went up the steps together. 'You rather stole my thunder,' he growled.

What a tremendous man he was. That whole weekend he could not have been kinder to the young idiot who had waved back at his supporters. For example, he showed me round those marvellous tapestries depicting the great battles of Blenheim, Ramilles, Oudenarde and Malplaquet. He told me who all the figures were, and how each battle turned out. Without Sir Winston putting me at my ease, I would gladly have allowed the earth to swallow me up.

CHAPTER 4

ONE PIP UP

I JOINED THE 9th Lancers at Hobart Barracks in Detmold, Northern Germany in the autumn of 1959, as the last officer to be commissioned into that Regiment. (On July 23rd 1960 it amalgamated with the 12th Lancers to become the 9th/12th Royal Lancers.)

It was normal for new young subalterns to be ignored completely by their fellow officers in the Mess. I had arrived with my pal, Charlie Hornby, and practically no one spoke to us at all for the first couple of weeks. This was extremely depressing. I went into the Officers Mess at about five o'clock on the day after I arrived. There was only one person in there (a Major) and he was reading a newspaper. He had a black labrador lying beside his chair, which sat up and wagged its tail when I entered. I went over and stroked it, at which point the Major growled 'Do you like dogs?'

'Yes, I do,' I replied.

'Well, get one of your own and stop bothering mine.'

One evening, Charlie and I decided to drown our sorrows; we reckoned that if nobody would acknowledge our existence, then we would try and have a good time on our own. We drank quantities of whisky, and at 9 o'clock, had a two-handed game of poker. I remember losing vast amounts of money to Charlie, and then passing out at about 10.30. He helped me to my room and put me into bed. I was in the left-hand of the three ground-floor bedrooms. In the middle was the adjutant, Nick Crossley, and in the further one was the senior unmarried major. He seemed to me older than God, but in actual fact I suppose he was about thirty-five. At 5 o'clock in the morning I woke up feeling very, very sick, so I staggered off to the loo at the end of the corridor. My head was throbbing, so my map reading was poor, and on my return journey I got into bed with the Major. Presumably he kicked me out, because by the time I had to rouse myself in the morning I was back in my own room.

I went down to the squadron office at the normal time, and soon after I got there the telephone rang – for me. On the other end was the adjutant, Captain Crossley. 'You must come up to my office immediately.' I had no recollection of what had gone on the night before and I merely thought to myself – well, finally someone is going to speak to me and ask me how I'm getting on. I went post-haste to the adjutant's office. 'Peto,' he said, 'what happened last night is too serious for me; the Commanding Officer wishes to see you.' I was then sent down the corridor, where I knocked on Colonel Laurie's door. 'Come in,' he said, 'do sit down. As you know your father is Colonel of this Regiment. It has been brought to my attention that you tried to sleep with one of your fellow officers last night. Are you perhaps a homosexual?' I really had no idea what he was talking about; but then in the back of my mind I started to remember that I had lost my way, and had got into the wrong bed early that morning. I replied 'No, Colonel, I am not a homosexual. I can remember now to what you are referring, and with great respect to the Major, if I had been that way inclined I would not have chosen him.' Luckily for me the matter was not taken any further, and my father was not informed. Nick Crossley was a great disciplinarian, and a perfect adjutant for this fine Regiment. No slip in standards was ever tolerated, and he was right – but he had a lovely human side as well. We have been firm friends for forty years.

I was allowed home for a month in the spring to practise for the Army Rackets Championship. The Regiment was required to send one officer for a week to Porton Down in Wiltshire, on a Gas Course and as a trade-off for my English trip it was decided that I was to be the 'volunteer'. It was an unbelievably unpleasant week, and we guinea-pigs were exposed to several types of gas, and nerve agent. But I had three weeks leave ahead of me, and the vile experience of Porton Down was soon a distant memory.

An old friend from Eton – I shall call him Wippy – had always told me that should I want a bed I could come and stay with him in Devonshire Street. On my first day in London, I found myself footloose and fancy free and thought I would walk past Wippy's flat to see if he was there. I knew this was most unlikely as he was working at the time for a bank. I rang the bell: no one came and I was just about to depart, when the door swung open and there was Wippy standing before me in a long Chinese dressing gown. 'Come in quickly,' he said. I went in and was about to ask him what on earth he was doing in his flat at 3 o'clock on a Friday afternoon, when he pre-empted me by saying 'Thank goodness you're here. Presumably having been in Germany for a while you will be feeling fairly randy. On my bed is a very large woman, and I

really don't think I can manage. Perhaps you can help out?'
We went into his bedroom and there, face down, was indeed
a huge lady. 'Wippy,' I said 'with the best will in the world, I
wouldn't know where to start.' He went next door to the bathroom, and a few moments later reappeared with a wet flannel
in his hand. He gave the lady a sharp flick across her buttocks
and made the immortal remark, 'Come on darling, fart and
give us a clue.'

It was during this time in London that I summoned up the
courage to ask a very pretty girl, whom I had met only once
before, out to dinner. Olda Willes was ravishing, and I felt the
evening went extremely well. I couldn't have been more
wrong. I made a lunge at Olda in the taxi after dinner, and
was summarily rebuffed. 'Me – kiss you? You're so wet, a puff
of wind would blow you over.' I was mortified, and my self-
esteem with the opposite sex, already low, sunk to rock bottom.

I went to Queens Club in West Kensington every day for
several hours, to play rackets with the resident Professional,
but other than that, my time was my own. The first weekend,
I asked some friends down to my parents' house near
Marlborough, to try and pick up the threads of English life
after five months in Germany. Among these was Henry
Lopes, whom I had originally met in Devonshire, and later at
Cothill, where we had arrived on the same day; we had gone
on to Eton together, so we knew each other extremely well.
Henry was as wild as a hawk, but enormous fun. He was guar-
anteed to liven up any house party. On the Saturday night we
played poker until the early hours. Henry had taken a shine
to Caroline, one of the girls who was staying. When the card

game finished he said to me 'I really like Caroline; would you mind very much if I went to say goodnight to her? Maybe you could tell me which room she is in?' I said, 'Henry, I asked Caroline down here because I hoped to make her my girl-friend. However, if you wish to visit her she is on the first floor, turn right and she is in the first bedroom on the right.' I went off to bed, slightly irritated, but soon fell asleep. The next morning I came down to breakfast, and my mother was sitting at the kitchen table. 'Good morning, darling', she said; then a little while later 'Do you think Henry is all right this morning?'

I said, 'I'm sure he's fine; why do you ask?'

'Well, it was very flattering last night, because he tried to get into bed with me. Maybe he mistook my room for his, although we *are* on different floors.'

At that moment we saw the figure of Henry darting out of the front of the house with his little suitcase, and hightailing it for his car. He was so embarrassed by what had gone on in the early hours that he couldn't face seeing my mother, and trying to explain the muddle he had got himself into. He simply left before we had even had breakfast.

In the middle of the following week, Henry telephoned me to say how sorry he was if he had upset my mother, and could he come the next weekend and try to redeem himself in her eyes? I rang home, and my father answered the telephone. I said I was hoping to have one or two people to stay the fol-lowing weekend. 'Fine' said my father, 'so long as you don't bring that fellow Henry.' I told him that, in fact, Henry was hoping to come, and after a while my father relented. We all arrived on the Saturday morning, and initially everything went well. However, long after my parents had gone to bed we crept up to our rooms on the second floor, and there Henry spotted a fire escape wheel, with a rope tied like a lasso on the side of the wall. 'I bet that hasn't been tested for ages', he said. With that, he put the noose round his waist, threw open the windows and hurtled as fast as he could out into the night. There was a scream from the reel on the wall, as if some enormous salmon was on the end of the line. Henry went about three yards straight out from the house and then came crashing back one floor down, directly through my father's dressing room window. He became impaled on the glass, and my father, covered in shards of glass himself, woke up and, in a daze, put on the light. What confronted him was a truly terrible sight – Henry, bleeding from head to toe in his white silk pyjamas and looking like Christ on the Cross. With great care we hauled him back to the second floor and patched him up, with my parents' help. It was some time before the poor fellow was allowed over the threshold again.

Germany in the late 1950s was considered a good posting for young officers. We played polo in the afternoons, and trained hard with the soldiers and our centurion tanks in the mornings. We also had to take these mighty vehicles on exercises and firing practice on the freezing Hohne ranges for up to three weeks at a time. However, during the weekends we used to make the occasional trip to Hamburg to see the nightlife (which was extremely exotic), and on other occasions I would drive with friends all the way to Munich and other major cities to sample life in those magnificent towns. My favourite haunt in sinful Hamburg was the Lausen Bar. The girls sat two or three to a table, with a flag of their country in front of each one indicating their nationality. In the middle of every table was an internal telephone. Punters like Rupert Lycett Green and myself would be shown to a large bar on our arrival. There we would have a drink or two while we cased the joint. When one had chosen a girl, one would telephone her from the bar, and ask her to come to an empty table on the other side of the dance floor. All very prim and proper, really. Rupert once persuaded one of these stunning girls to travel north with him to Travemunde in his ferret scout car. They had a splendid night, winning at the casino, and not getting much sleep thereafter. He returned the lady behind her correct flag the following evening. One night, I was enjoying a very slow smooch with an Italian girl. My reverie was rudely interrupted, when I heard the voice of our ultra-correct Second-in-Command hissing in his lady's ear: 'Any more of this familiarity, and the fuck's off.'

Peter and Veronica Munster, who lived at Schlöss Derneburg, near Hildesheim, were unbelievable in their generosity to young officers stationed in Northern Germany. I used to go there at least once a month and the houseparties were huge fun. We played cards, danced and sometimes even made amateur James Bond films. We also shot a few pigs. We drank vodka which Peter brewed commercially in his own still. Nothing seemed to faze our hosts and laughter and happiness were the name of the game.

The time flew by, and soon the whole Regiment was due to return to Tidworth in June of 1960, to prepare for our amalgamation with the 12th Lancers. My father was our honorary Colonel, and he was to come out at the end of May to take the final overseas parade in the 245-year history of our Regiment. Endless polishing and practising went on before his arrival, and I was chosen to be in command of the Lance Guard of Honour. It was a wonderful occasion and everything went off beautifully, except that I had persuaded the Bandmaster to change the tune to which my father inspected his Lance Guard. I felt sure that the song I chose would be unknown to him, but would make some of the soldiers smile. How wrong I was, because when he started his inspection and the tune *My Old Man's a Dustman* was struck up by the band, my father murmured to me 'Nicholas, I will see you after the parade.' Luckily the whole day was such a success, that he was able to smile and forgive at the end of it.

There was a lull for about three weeks after this parade before we actually embarked for England. Rupert Lycett Green asked me one day whether I would like a dancing lesson from him. I knew that he was a superb dancer, particularly good at jiving to fast music. I knew also that I had no idea, and I felt very gauche when I went to parties, being such a poor performer. I accepted his offer in good faith, and he did spend half-an-hour during NAAFI break on three consecutive mornings, teaching me the basics. I can even remember the music to which we danced; it was invariably Louis Prima and Keeley Smith – the songs we liked most were *Embraceable You* and *Those falling Leaves drift by my Window, those autumn leaves of red and gold.* At the end of the three days he said, 'Right, you're good enough at that; now would you like to learn to play poker properly?' I accepted this offer in good faith also and on the first morning I was allowed to win a few marks, but during the next couple of weeks I lost heavily. It was only then that I realised Rupert had set me up with the dancing lessons to gain my confidence, always having the ulterior motive of winning money off me at the poker table. However, in the long run it stood me in good stead. I have had great fun playing this game, and because of those tough early lessons I have held my own over the years in some very large poker schools. In 1970, I was runner-up to Stuart Wheeler in the British Poker Championships. An added bonus was that Rupert ended up as a close friend and confidante.

We all arrived back at Tidworth in June 1960 to prepare for our final parade when our Colonel-in-Chief, Her Majesty Queen Elizabeth the Queen Mother, would present the 9th Lancer Guidon. As this would be the last parade of the Regiment we were determined that it should be the best ever. July 23rd was a beautiful sunny day and none of us who took part will ever forget it. The Regiment, led by Captain Nick Crossley, our Adjutant, who was mounted on his grey charger, marched on parade to the tune of *Old Comrades*. It was a magnificent sight. The guards were dressed in blue with silver collar badges backed by a red patch, white gloves and red and yellow full dress girdles. The lance flags fluttering in the gentle breeze added colour to this splendid scene. The Bandsmen were in full dress. The scarlet trumpet banners showed up brilliantly. Lieutenant Colonel David Laurie MC, the Commanding Officer, rode on and took over the parade. A fanfare was blown, kettle drums and banners were marched on parade to the Regimental Trot. The Regimental flag was broken behind the dais and at that moment a scarlet helicopter circled overhead; Her Majesty arrived at precisely 11 am.

The whole Guidon Parade went like clockwork, and was the culmination of the long and distinguished history since the Regiment was raised. There were six hundred and fifty people at the buffet luncheon in the Officers Mess tent, a vast marquee erected on the lawn.

But I had a worry on my mind. I had run up a very nasty bill with my bookmaker, and by mid-July I owed him £320. It doesn't sound much now, but in 1960 it was a fortune (roughly equivalent to my annual pay as a 2nd Lieutenant). The great filly *Petite Etoile* was running in The King George at Ascot on July 16th. She had never been beaten, and I believed she was a certainty. Ridden by Lester Piggott, she started at 2-5 on. With a great deal of persuasion my bookie accepted my bet of £1000 to win £400. This would sort out my problem, with £80 to spare, I thought, much relieved.

As the race unfolded, Lester appeared to be cruising on the grey filly. At the furlong pole she accelerated into second place just behind the leader *Aggressor*, ridden by Jimmy Lindley. Slowly, slowly she gathered in *Aggressor*, but now the finishing post was looming. With fifty yards to go *Petite Etoile* was still half a length adrift. Lester was hard at work, but she had no more to offer in the soft ground. I was done for: now I owed £1320. At the end of July, at my wit's end, I telephoned my sister's husband Ronnie Murphy. A charming Irishman, Ronnie, and he knows the ups and downs of racing like few others. 'Don't give it a thought,' he said from his home in County Cork. 'I'll send you the money, and you can pay me back whenever.' What an amazing fellow to do that – I shall never forget it.

CHAPTER 5

TWO DOZEN
WHITE MICE

TIDWORTH HAD BEEN a splendid posting for me, since it was so close to my home at Lockeridge. But in the autumn of 1960 the Regiment was sent to Northern Ireland. Most of the soldiers went to Omagh in County Tyrone, but C Squadron, which I was in, went straight to Castle Archdale on the banks of Loch Erne in County Fermanagh. Although the IRA were active, their atrocities had not yet begun in earnest; they were more of a nuisance, and could be contained by a show of force. We were due to remain in Northern Ireland for about two years, and so there was every opportunity to involve ourselves in local life. Willy Bulwer-Long and I both bought horses to hunt, and made innumerable forays to the South. We hunted a great deal with the Duhallow in County Cork and also with the Limerick. I became friendly with a girl called Moira Pilkington who lived in the Meath country at Stackallan. Accordingly, I took my horse down there and had several days hunting with her as well. The girls in the South were mostly excellent riders, braver and more proficient at crossing the country than I was, so my pursuit of Moira, and her friend Althea Urquhart, was inevitably a frustrating pastime in the hunting field. Willy had fallen for the daughter of the Duhallow MFH, Ginny Freeman Jackson. She was an

Olympic rider and extremely good looking – an irresistible combination. These ladies were all very wild but tremendous fun, mostly still in their teens.

We decided to give a Regimental Dance in our Mess at Omagh, and of course invited all our new friends and contacts from over the border. The party was not entirely to the liking of Moira and Althea – I suspect they thought it was not great craic, a dull affair – and so they decided to leave early and set off home. Since they were meant to be staying the night with one of the married officers, they had no means of transport. However, somehow Althea managed to start one of our three-ton lorries, and the two of them took off at about two in the morning. Before they left the Mess, they had played what might have been a very expensive practical joke. They went around the bathrooms, and put all the plugs in the baths and basins. They then turned the taps on slowly, and departed. I knew nothing about this of course, and went off to bed at about the same time as they left. Their journey to the border was uneventful, despite being in an army lorry, though of course they were stopped by the military when they arrived at the crossing point. Our Duty Officer was immediately telephoned, to be told that there were two girls in long evening dresses who had hijacked one of the 9th/12th Lancer lorries. He said they were hoping to get to their home near Dublin. I was immediately woken, and luckily went into one of the bathrooms to wash my face before setting off to see what was happening. There I was confronted by a couple of inches of water, and I saw immediately that all the taps were running in the baths and basins. I hurtled round and turned everything off, pulling out the plugs at the same time. Had I not been woken up, and had the water continued to run until morning, I cannot imagine the damage which would have ensued. Probably the ceilings would have collapsed onto the tables and chairs and marvellous carpets below, many of which had been brought back from India between the two Wars. As it was, a mopping-up operation was put into place immediately, with a dozen soldiers armed with buckets and squeegees. By the time I got to the border, the girls had hitched a lift and disappeared down to the South. Their antics were hushed up, luckily for me, and there were no repercussions. I pursued Moira relentlessly, both out hunting and at dances, for the next six months. I made very little progress, which of course made me all the more eager.

While I was in the small barracks at Castle Archdale I had as my neighbour in the next bedroom, Hew Kennedy, the fellow who had emptied a bucket of boiling water over my back a couple of years earlier at Sandhurst. By this stage he was a collector of armour and old weaponry. One evening I was lying on my bed reading, when there was a tremendous BANG and I saw a large hole which had been blown through the thin plywood. Hew had been testing one of his old rifles; I imagine he thought it definitely would not fire. Not only did the gun go off, but the bullet shot through three adjacent bedroom walls. Nobody was hurt, but it seemed to me that the sooner he and I went our separate ways the safer it would be for me. For the most part, however, one's Regiment is an exclusive confraternity. Our lives revolved around those of our fellow officers, and the soldiers of one's Troop became one's family. Each man was very important to his officer; you knew them inside out, and vice versa.

The hospitality shown to us by local landowners was incredible. Harry and Camilla Erne at Crom Castle, on the banks of Lough Erne, asked us to shoot, to water-ski, and to dinner unstintingly. In due course he became my brother-in-law for a while, because I married Camilla's sister Lucinda. In later years Harry had several close encounters with the IRA. His lovely estate was right on the border, at Newtown Butler, and he was an obvious target. Possibly his most fortunate escape was from the Enniskillen Bomb on 8th November 1987. As Lord Lieutenant of Fermanagh, Harry was due to take the salute at the annual Remembrance Day service. The Chief Constable had gone to collect him, and they lingered a few minutes over their cups of coffee. They had not quite taken up their positions on the dais when the huge bomb exploded at two minutes to eleven.

The horrific carnage of the immediate aftermath was caught on amateur video footage, and it shocked the world. The Provisional IRA, who were responsible, lost support from that moment, and the eleven people killed may not have died in vain, as this outrage was undoubtedly a turning point. Charles Caulfield was named in the House of Commons as the mastermind behind the bombing; he has still not been brought to book.

James Hamilton, at Baron's Court told us we could go over there whenever we wished. I was meandering down the long drive on my first visit, for lunch, came to a fork in the road, and had no idea which way to go. I spotted an old retainer in a well-worn woolly, kneeling under a huge rhododendron. I beckoned him over, and asked him the way to the big house. 'If you don't mind a muddy fellow in your car, I'll hop in and direct you. I'm going up there myself.' We sped away, and arrived a few minutes later. As we went in my passenger said, 'So sorry, I haven't introduced myself. I'm the Duke of Abercorn. You must be one of James's young army friends.'

Early in our tour I was taking my Troop out on a patrol along the border. My corporal, driving the front scout car, rounded a sharp bend on a narrow little road and ran straight into a hearse coming the other way, with dramatic effect. The three vehicles behind it all shunted into each other, and there was much swearing, gesticulating and shouting from the funeral cortège – this despite the fact we were only going about three or four miles an hour. We reported the incident on our return to barracks, and a fortnight later word came down from military headquarters in Belfast that we were not to take our vehicles out again, except in an emergency. It was deemed that they were too large for the Northern Ireland roads, and in order to prevent further incidents we were instructed to keep them in the barracks. This suited us troop leaders perfectly, because all we could then do was maintain the scout cars and armoured cars, and start them up each morning to make sure they were in tip top working order. By about 9 o'clock these tasks were completed, and the rest of the day was normally ours to do what we liked with. As a result I could make a dash in my car for a Meet of one of the packs of foxhounds, either locally or in the South, depending on what I had planned.

We clubbed together and bought a small speedboat which we berthed on Loch Erne. One of our officers, Alec Montgomerie, was a brilliant snow skier (he represented England in the Olympics), and so water skiing came very easily to him. We laid out a line of slalom buoys, and within a month even I became fairly proficient. Alec was by far the best of us; he was able to cut the water with his shoulder on each turn, and was a joy to watch.

Another subaltern who became a lifelong friend was Charles Enderby. He was mad on shooting, and he and I travelled far and wide to explore the possibilities Northern Ireland had to offer. We found many marvellous bogs around Loch Erne and the other nearby lochs, which were full of snipe and duck and had enormous fun; we both had dogs to help retrieve what we shot. We became friendly with a splendid man called Dick Hermon. He was a superb shot – the best I've ever seen – and he knew everything there was to know about the sport in our part of the Province, since he had lived there for many years. Major Hermon was extremely modest about his prowess, but action speaks louder than words. In 1936, urged on by a friend, he walked in reluctantly off the street and won the Daily Telegraph British clay-pigeon championship, beating the world champion in the process – and this with a borrowed gun. He had never fired at a clay before, and he won with a record score. He repeated the feat the following year, and never fired at another clay-pigeon for the rest of his life, declaring it boring. With the Guinness family he shot 100 woodcock to his own gun on three successive days. Shooting pigeon at Tynan Abbey from a high tower he shot 286 birds with 300 cartridges in a howling gale.

It was Dick who took us to Classibawn. Lord Mountbatten, the owner, was mainly an absentee landlord, at least during the winter months. Dick had a very Irish arrangement with the gamekeeper, which seemed to be that provided the Laird was not in residence we could come and try our luck wild fowling. Charles and I would set out early, when the bushes were shaggy with hoar frost, and we had some very exciting days. We often saw several thousand geese and masses of different types of ducks. We were never more than four guns shooting, and a typical bag would be a couple of geese, twenty-five assorted ducks, two or three pheasants, some snipe, and maybe half a dozen woodcock. I once shot a cock grouse there – I don't suppose one has been seen in that part of Ireland from that day to this.

The Regiment organised cross-country races for all the neighbouring riding enthusiasts and ourselves, over natural obstacles, of which there were any number dividing the small fields that are so common on the farms of the North. The Fermanagh Harriers was our local pack of hounds and it was at their point-to-point that I had my first ride in a race. Although I rode in several point-to-points, both in Northern Ireland and England, I only won one race, on a horse of mine called *Solway Prince*.

One spring evening I stopped with my soldiers at the Top Hat Ballroom in Lisnaskea, a little village in County Fermanagh. There were several bicycles and cars outside, so we realised there was probably a dance going on. In we went, and surveyed the scene. On a row of benches to the left were twenty or so girls, while milling around the bar (which only sold soft drinks) were about half-a-dozen young lads. Some of my soldiers started dancing with the girls, and having an enjoyable time. After a while Trooper Patey, a handsome fellow, came up to me and said 'Come on Sir, why don't you choose a girl and have a dance?' I walked down the row of young ladies, in my mind pretty sure that they were all longing to dance with this young uniformed officer. I picked out the least unattractive girl and said 'Would you like to dance with me?' From her position on the bench she very slowly looked me up, down and then up again, and replied in her broad Northern Irish accent, 'Why don't you try dancin' with my sister, she's sweatin' less?' This goes to show that even in 1962 there was a strong anti-British feeling in the North – or was it just that she didn't fancy me?

One of the potentially more exacting exercises which the hierarchy dreamt up for the Senior NCOs and young officers was to make us find our way from Omagh to a Barracks just outside Belfast. The Parachute Regiment was to be the enemy, and would search for us. We all had to set off on our own, and were disqualified if we were caught using a road or a vehicle. The Paras had helicopters, and any number of tough soldiers, who set up road blocks and combed the whole area. I had a friend, Marcus Macausland, who had a timber business. I persuaded him to hide me under a large lorry-load of railway sleepers, and during the night he drove me to within a couple of miles of my destination. The lorry had been stopped and searched by torchlight at one of the barricades, but I remained undiscovered. I slipped out of my scary little cubicle, and made haste for the rendezvous with the aid of my compass. First man home, no questions asked, and many brownie points. A few years later Marcus was horribly tortured, and subsequently murdered, by the IRA.

It was in July 1962 that Willy Bulwer-Long, Charlie Hornby and I decided to rent a little house on the edge of Dublin for the Horse Show week. We asked our respective girlfriends to stay, and we 'borrowed' a couple of corporals from the officers' mess to look after us. On the Sunday evening at the commencement of proceedings, we gave a cocktail party in our garden. About eighty people came, nearly all in their early twenties, and they seemed to have a good time. Ten of us then went out to dinner at the Gresham Hotel, and returned home at midnight. At one end of our rented house there had been a lovely conservatory, and even in the middle of the night we couldn't help noticing that it was no longer there. The next morning as daylight broke we went to see what had happened. Glass from the conservatory was spread all over the lawn, and there were pieces of flesh liberally scattered amongst the debris. When I rang the lady who owned the house she was naturally upset about her conservatory. Then she told me that she had three peacocks which roosted on its beam each evening. Someone had come while we were away at dinner and had blown up the glasshouse and, sadly, the peacocks as well.

This episode remained an unsolved mystery for nearly thirty years. It was only in 1990 when I was staying the weekend in Yorkshire that I rediscovered Pete Petersham. Late one evening he said to me 'Did you get a large bill when you took that house for the Dublin Horse Show back in 1962?' I said 'Yes, I certainly did. My bill for damages was four times the size of the week's rent, and we had to replace three peacocks which also died in the explosion.' 'Oh dear,' said Pete, 'If I had known they were there I wouldn't have blown the place up.' I said to him 'Why on earth did you do it?' 'Well,' he said, 'although I was only in my teens when you had your party, both my sisters, Jane and Avena, were going and I was furious that you had not asked me – so I decided to do something about it, to leave my mark.' Pete was possibly the wildest of all the wild men of the South of Ireland; one could write a book just about his antics.

My memories of that Horse Show week are mainly blurred, but two other things do still stand out. On the Tuesday night, there was a Ball at the Shelbourne Hotel, to which we went. It was thrown by a rich Irish lady on behalf of her daughter (whom we did not know). On the way back from the Horse Show that afternoon I stopped off at a Pet Store and bought two dozen white mice. My next port of call was the shop two doors down, a tobacconists. There I got masses of pipe cleaners. I then went to the local milliner where I purchased a few yards of white silk. I spent the evening cutting up the silk, and with the aid of the pipe cleaners made parachutes for the white mice. Charlie, Willy and I set off for the dance at about 10 o'clock that evening, and in our pockets we each had half-a-dozen of the little fellows. Above the dance floor at the Shelbourne there is a balcony, and it was there we went. When the dancing was in full swing we attached the mice to the pipe cleaners and parachuted them down on the revellers below. Of course, the early 1960s were the days of the beehive hairdo, and one or two mice had direct hits. They were only loosely attached by their harnesses, so that on landing they scrabbled away pretty fast. There was complete pandemonium below, and the three of us left our eyrie and went downstairs to join the dancers, most of whom were saying 'Who on earth could have ruined the party by doing this?' We joined them in their remonstrations.

It was following that dance that the three of us decided to go for a water ski. We had trailed the speedboat down behind one of our cars and had anchored it in the local harbour. At about two in the morning we set off and each had a short ski, the idea being that it would sober us up, and in this it was successful. We returned to the mooring, and tied the boat to the wall. After breakfast the next day, we wandered down to the harbour on our way to the Horse Show, to make sure that all was in order. We realised that something might be amiss when we saw a small crowd of locals at exactly the place where we had tied up. Of course, during the ensuing time the tide had ebbed, and there was our beloved speedboat attached by a flimsy piece of string to a small bolt in the sea wall; it was dangling with its bow pointing to the sky, and its stern about thirty feet above the rocks below. There was nothing to be done but to return later that afternoon when the tide had come in. Thank goodness the little piece of twine held, and we were able to rescue our vessel.

I had recently become very attracted to an incredibly beautiful girl called Kari Shepherd. She was tall and blonde, with a wonderful figure, in much demand as a model and the daughter of Gay Shepherd, who was the clerk of several National Hunt racecourses, and a very well known man in the racing world. Kari and I went out with each other for three years, and she was an unbelievably loyal girlfriend. All through my next posting, when the Regiment was sent to the Middle East, Kari wrote me one or two letters a week, which did wonders for my morale when I was so far from home. C Squadron, of which I was still one of the Troop Leaders, was bound for Sharjah – in those days a relatively unknown State on the Persian Gulf, between Dubai and Muscat, which was bounded on its eastern side by the Arabian Sea.

The Brothers Meeting. Chedington Court 15th December 1915

The Seven Sons of Sir Morton Peto Bt.

Standing from left to right: Samuel, Harold, Morton (jnr), Mary (Henry's wife) and Frank; seated from left to right: Basil, Henry and Herbert.

My great-grandfather was Sir Morton Peto of Somerleyton (1808-1889). He was an eminent Victorian railway entrepreneur, philanthropist and MP for Norwich. He was the contractor who built Nelson's column, rebuilt a large section of the Houses of Parliament and built railways all over the world. He was created a baronet for his part in the construction of the Crimea Railway. Also in this picture is Harold (1854-1933), an architect and famous landscape garden designer. Several of his gardens still live on – Iford Manor, Somerset, where he lived, Buscot in Gloucestershire, Heale House in Wiltshire and Garinish Island off County Cork. My grandfather, Basil (1862-1945), was the youngest of Sir Morton's fifteen children. He was MP for Hungerford and then for Barnstaple and was created a baronet in 1927. This title passed to my brother, Michael in 1980.

Wendy, Mike, NP. Camberley, 1941.

Cothill House Cricket Colours, 1952. From left to right: Henry Lopes,
Seton Wills, Henry Berens, NP, Michael Abel Smith

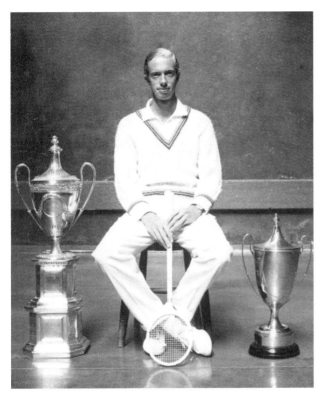

NP with Army Rackets
Doubles and Singles
Trophies, 1963.

NP in Sharjah, 1963.

Front row, from left to right: Stoker Hartington, NP, Sophy Cavendish, Debo Devonshire, Emma Tennant; second row, from left to right: Lady Dorothy Macmillan, Mary Ann Parker Bowles, Harold Macmillan, Amanda Heywood Lonsdale, Theresa Keswick, Christopher Balfour, Anne and Tom Egerton, Toby Tennant; third row, from left to right: Lady Mersey, Anne and Derek Parker Bowles, Elizabeth Wright, Davina Lloyd, Nanny, Laura Cecil; fourth and fifth rows, from left to right: Ric Beckett, Kate Fleming, Robert Pilkington, Lord Mersey, Neil Balfour, Hugh Cecil, Hamish Leslie Melville, Mark Fisher, Simon Head, Mike Tollemache and Andrew Parker Bowles.

Chips and Sarah Keswick's wedding, 1966, the ushers. From left to right: Jamie Ramsay, Charlie Lyell, Simon Keswick, Henry Lopes, NP, Stoker Hartington, Bobby Corbett, Charles Spencer-Churchill, Anthony Ramsay.

Jake Morley at Charlie and Amanda Hornby's Wedding, 1967.

Off to Ascot Races from Blenheim Palace, June 1964. Back row from left to right: Aureol Mackeson-Sandbach, Simon Parker Bowles, Bobby Corbett, Charles Spencer-Churchill, Mary Ann Parker Bowles, Chips Keswick; front row from left to right: Michael Saintangelo, Serena Russell, Mimi Russell, Gill Fuller, NP.

NP and Simon Keswick with two friends at the Georgian Pussy Club, 1963.

At the musical *Hair*, February 1970. Bottom of picture from left: Anne Peto, NP, HRH Princess Anne, Andrew Parker Bowles.

NP and Anne, 1970.

Stoker Hartington paddling across the Blackwater at Careysville, 1970.

CHAPTER 6

PLAYING IN THE SAND

SHARJAH WAS TO be my home from the end of September 1962 until C Squadron was relieved in April 1963. It had the advantage of being 1500 miles from Regimental Headquarters (in Aden), and only in contact through the daily radio call. We had excellent accommodation, which we shared with a squadron of the Royal Air Force and a contingent of Trucial Oman Scouts. When there was time for relaxation, a swimming pool and cinema were on hand and a saddle club provided riding and polo, which we played on the salt flats, washing down our ponies afterwards in the sea. However, the operational and training demands on troops were continuous. Long distance patrols to Muscat and Oman, Qatar, Buraimi and elsewhere often lasted up to three weeks, and sometimes covered over a thousand miles. My Squadron Leader, Major Gatensbury, was content to let us young officers have a free rein, and we gained enormous experience taking our soldiers so far into the desert, and at times across some of the most unforgiving terrain on earth, known as the 'empty quarter'. Here there was no chance of finding water, and the daytime temperature often rose to 130°F, appalling conditions for both men and machines. The engines of our scout cars, which anyway ran near boiling point, often seized up, or gave up the ghost in this scorching, shimmering heat. One could crack open an egg on the bonnet, and it would fry in a matter of seconds.

There was always a wind blowing along the high dunes; the sand billowing off their sharp ridges continually changed the shape of their tops. One's tracks were covered in minutes, and the compass was one's lifeline. On the occasional clear, still nights I was struck by the incredible brightness of the stars – far brighter than at home.

I made friends with a couple of the RAF pilots, one of whom, Harry, mentioned to me one day that he and two others were taking their three fighters to Delhi on a training run. 'Would you like to come?' he said. 'I could take you if you lie down beside me.' I thought it sounded tremendous fun, so of course I jumped at the chance. It was an exhilarating, but terrifying experience. I lay on my stomach as we hurtled towards India, and my insides seemed to be trailing along several yards behind my body. On our arrival, I had time for a walk around their Mess and a quick cup of tea, and was then told that I must get back in the plane as we were returning immediately. I don't suppose many people have made a specific trip to India for a shorter time, or seen less of the country. About a month later Harry flew his fighter into the side of a mountain just after take-off from Sharjah. What went wrong I never knew, but it was a great shock to all of his friends who lived in that tight-knit circle.

It is hard now to believe that in 1962 there was no oil gushing from the Sharjah desert, or indeed from Dubai or any of the United Arab Emirates. No roads, just sand tracks, and very few proper buildings – just masses of bedouin-type tents.

Peter Glenapp was one of our young officers. His father was Chairman of a large company, Inchcape, which traded in the Middle and Far East. One of their Arab clients, wishing to gain favour, presented Peter with a skiboat while he was with us in Sharjah. We would water-ski at dawn on the creek in front of our buildings. The wash created both by the boat turning and the water-skiier's movements splashed briskly onto the shore, much to the fury of the local tribeswomen, who came down in their black shawls with their faces covered, to do their ablutions every morning on the edge of the water. Sometimes we made them a little wetter than they anticipated.

At that time I had the most marvellous sergeant with me, Jack Suckling. He was a constant rock and a man with a splendid sense of humour, yet tremendous judgement. He and I and the rest of my troop, which consisted of fourteen soldiers and a corporal, went on a long patrol down to Muscat. We stopped at little villages on the way, where it was as if time had stood still for several hundred years. Ibri was a beautiful oasis village, with magnificent palm trees, and a crystal clear sparkling stream running through its centre. We met a local leader called the Wali of Dhank who had about fifteen retainers, all armed to the teeth. We made our way down to Muscat across the desert and at times over very mountainous terrain. On our return, we travelled for the most part along the shore of the Arabian Sea. Each morning we would have a swim in the very warm water, and boil it up for a shave before breakfast. On patrols like this our supplies were brought to us by Thirteen Flight Army Air Corps, and it was always exciting to see one of their little aircraft popping over the horizon. I remember hoping against hope that there would be letters from England, and particularly from Kari. One of our pilots, Major Lewis, was tragically killed when his aeroplane crashed on landing near the Buraimi Oasis, during an appalling sand storm, of the type which could blow up in minutes, with no warning at all. Their density was frightening, and the sand penetrated one's mouth, eyes, nose, clothing – every single orifice.

At the end of January 1963 I was allowed home for a month's leave in order, once again, to try and win the Army Rackets Championships. This was unbelievably good of my superiors, and I only hoped that I would not let them down. I had been a finalist in the three previous years, but had never managed to win. It was wonderful being back in England again, seeing my parents, my friends and of course Kari Shepherd. I practised for the tournament very hard, using the Marlborough Rackets Court, since it was close to our home. I reached the final without too much problem, and on Saturday the 23rd February I walked onto the court to try, for the fourth time, to win the final. I was playing against Michael Dunning, whom I knew well; I also knew that he was a gifted player. I managed to beat him three sets to love, lucky to strike form at the right moment. *The Times* correspondent said I had 'an easy, fluent style with great power and diversity of stroke.' I was simply thrilled to have won, and in the afternoon Anthony Williams and I won the doubles competition as well. So I returned to Aden the following day with photographs of two enormous cups, and a letter of congratulations from our Colonel-in-Chief, Queen Elizabeth the Queen Mother.

In April 1963 C Squadron was recalled to Aden and in the following month I was sent with my troop to Mukerias, a permanent tented camp, which was three thousand feet up, and two miles from the Yemen border. This was a time when the new Ruler of the Yemen, supported by Colonel Nasser of Egypt, was trying to forge a union with Aden, a scenario that had all the ingredients for a classic colonial confrontation. There were rapidly increasing numbers of incidents along the frontier between the Yemen and Aden – a newly defined border, mostly way up in the hills – and soon after arriving at Mukerias I was told to go to Beihan, where tribesmen had crossed the frontier and occupied part of a village called Hagar. They had with them some field guns, heavy machine guns, mortars, and any number of rifles and supporters. The Yemeni were (and are) fearless fighters who would stop at nothing. No torture for their captives was considered too unpleasant. Only the previous week I had been told of a man being found strapped to a stake by the roadside. He had been castrated, and his balls had been sewn crudely into his mouth.

After a rapid night march I deployed my boys at dawn, supported by the Royal Horse Artillery. A punchy little battle followed, during which my Saladin armoured car fired forty shells, and the RHA fired a hundred and eighty rounds. The village was destroyed and our enemy, who had bravely manned a mud fort till it crumbled around them, withdrew. Later that day I went with a couple of soldiers to look at the damage first hand. There I found eight dead Yemeni tribesmen. To quote from the Regimental History: '5 Troop, C Squadron, (Lt Peto) was deployed at dawn, and a very spirited fire-fight followed. This engagement was the most warlike that any troop of the Regiment experienced during the tour.'

Every night for the next two weeks some of the tribesmen would come over the border after dark, and in commando-style try to infiltrate my position. They would then fire at random at our vehicles, hoping to get their own back. One of my soldiers was shot in the arm, but otherwise we were undamaged. What frightened me more than the Yemeni, were the enormous camel spiders which came out to feed at night. Once, I awoke under my mosquito net, and there was a camel spider directly above my face, stationary on the net. It was only about three inches away from my skin, and it was so big that it blocked out the full moon above it.

While I was up-country in Beihan I suddenly became very ill. I was losing a lot of weight extremely quickly and falling in and out of consciousness. One of our little aircraft flew me down to Aden, where I was taken straight to the military hospital. I was diagnosed with some form of bilharzia and was critical for seven or eight days, by which stage my weight had gone from twelve and a half stone to nine and a half. All I remember was waking up one day to find a large WRAC matron towering over me. 'You do realise', she said to me in a strident voice, 'there is no cure for this disease. Half the people who catch it die, and the other half go mad.' A cure was not found for this condition until 1982, but, amazingly after about a month of illness, I did make a full recovery.

In the evenings, I sometimes drove to the Mess of the Royal Scots Greys for dinner and a game of poker and it was here that I struck up a lasting friendship with Duncan Davidson (he of the fictitious student dance I mentioned earlier). The Regiment was to move when our year was up in September 1963 to Osnabrück in Germany. Just before leaving Aden, I bought myself an Alfa Romeo Sprint – bright red and a convertible – which I thought was the 'bee's knees'. I had it shipped home ahead of me and even after paying tax to bring it to England my total bill was only £1100. A year later I turned it over in the newly-built Knightsbridge underpass. The car was a write-off, but I sustained only bruising and two broken ribs.

I also brought back with me five beautiful South Arabian alabaster funerary heads which I had bought from a trader on the Yemen border. They were particularly fine and dated from the First Century BC. Each one cost me £5. (Soon after we left the country, trading in this sort of object was outlawed.) I sold my hoard at Christies in January 1964, and I received a cheque for £800. I wonder what they would be worth today.

CHAPTER 7

A LITTLE GREEN PLASTIC FROG

BETWEEN OUR MIDDLE EASTERN posting and arrival in Osnabrück in Germany we were allowed two months leave in the UK. Kari Shepherd and I had gone our separate ways, and I had a new girlfriend, Mary Ann Parker Bowles, who lived with her parents and brothers, Andrew, Simon and Ric, just outside Newbury. One spring day, Mary Ann took me fishing on the river Kennet with her friend and neighbour Gerald Ward. We wandered up the river bank, while I tried to impress her with my knowledge of how to catch trout with a dry fly. But I could not get any fish to show an interest, and I realised that as lunch time approached, I was going to have nothing to show for my efforts. In desperation, I took off my dry fly and put on a little plastic frog, which I happened to have with me. I flicked this upstream and slowly jerked it back under the nearside bank. There was a mighty commotion. I had hooked a large trout, which I eventually landed, before we went back to the lunch hut – to find that no one else had caught anything. They were very impressed with my four pound fish, and Aylmer Tryon – a brilliant fisherman – asked me what I had caught it on. I was about to lie that I had been using a lightly dressed Blue Dunn, when Mary Ann produced my green frog from her bag, popped it onto her side plate and, pushing it across towards Aylmer said, 'Isn't he clever? He couldn't get anything the normal way, so he put on this little chap.' To use such a thing on a beautiful chalk stream like the Kennet was unbelievably bad form, and both Gerald and Aylmer gave me a thorough dressing down.

Ascot Races came around, and Mary Ann and I were asked to Blenheim for the week, where we had an amazing time, with a large number of servants looking after us all. One of our friends who was also a guest, Bobby Corbett, ran out of money trying to tip the various footmen on his departure. As he headed towards his little car, Mr Wadman, the Head Butler, opened its door for him and in desperation Bobby felt in his pockets to see if there was anything left. He found a crumpled ten shilling note and handed it to Mr Wadman, mumbling 'Thank you very much for looking after me so well.' Mr Wadman took the note, unravelled it slowly, and then handed it back to Bobby, quietly saying 'I think, Mr Bobby, your need may well be greater than mine.' One of nature's bachelors, Bobby was a unique character, extremely well read, charming, and with a formidable command of the English language. Sadly he died before he was sixty. He left us with a final smile by designing his own headstone. There is a fox cut into the top, and the words: 'The Honourable Robert Cameron Corbett MFH' and at the bottom is engraved: 'Here I lie, prostrate as usual'.

Serena Russell, the stunning grand-daughter of the Duke of Marlborough, had brought her boyfriend Michael Saintangelo, to whom she had recently announced her engagement. Bert Marlborough didn't like the idea of her marrying this swarthy Italian, and gave him a hard time.

'What did you say your name was?'

'Saintangelo, Sir.'

'One of my footmen has the same name: you are probably related to him.'

The marriage never did take place. Serena became a life-long friend of mine. After her husband died she married the dashing Neil Balfour, in 1979; their hospitality is legendary and there is only one man I know who has as many friends as Neil – his brother Christopher, a charming, amusing and gregarious life-enhancer.

Mary Ann Parker Bowles was a very beautiful girl, and also a strong Roman Catholic. She took me to a dance in the Corn Market in Newbury one night and I felt that things had gone so well that this might be my moment to make a move. We went home at about midnight, just before the rest of the house party and I wandered down the long passage from my spare room to Mary Ann's bedroom. Unknown to me her father was coming up the drive and could see my progress in his headlights as I passed each window. I heard him racing up the back stairs as I was about to enter Mary Ann's room. I shot into the nearest loo and locked the door. Derek Parker Bowles came up the stairs two at a time, and rattled on the handle. 'I know you're in there,' he said menacingly, 'come out immediately.' I sat on the lavatory seat, petrified. Eventually I emerged sheepishly and Derek said, 'What on earth do you think you are doing down this end of the house?'

'Just going to the bathroom.'

'Well,' he said, 'let me show you five lavatories that are nearer your bedroom than this one.'

Soon after this episode, Mary Ann deserted me for Gerald Ward, so I had to look for pastures new.

Gerald's sister died when she was in her fifties, by which time she had been married nine times. Her second husband was a vast chap with closely cropped hair, whom we nicknamed Oddjob. One day at Ogbourne Golf Club he and Gerald challenged Richard Haslem, the professional, and me to a game. I couldn't believe my luck when they agreed to play for fifty pounds. As we stood on the first tee and discussed our handicaps, I was mortified to hear Oddjob say he was scratch. He didn't look as if he could possibly be a great golfer. He was; Richard and I took a beating.

It was while I was at home on holiday that I heard I was to be an ADC to General Norman Wheeler in Germany, rather than returning to my Regiment. General Wheeler was a delightful man in the Royal Ulster Rifles. I spent a year as his ADC, and during that time we travelled extensively throughout northern Germany, visiting all the Regiments under his command, using both staff car and helicopter. We spent a week in Paris at the SHAPE Conference, and went as far afield as Potsdam and Berlin. I got on well with his wife Helen but I did have a lot of difficulty with his daughter who used to order me around as if I was her personal lackey – this I resented. Otherwise, it was a very easy time for me, far more so than serving with the Regiment in Osnabrück. By this stage I had a splendid new girlfriend called Magda Stirling, and she came to visit me for a week during the army skiing championships at Oberjöch in January 1965. Magda and I had a wonderful year together, even though I was mainly based in Germany. I used to fly back one weekend a month to

stay with her at her parents' home in Scotland, or occasionally in her flat in Edinburgh where she was studying.

Magda's mother, Susie, never saw my point, and we had
several dramatic run-ins. The worst of these was over one of
her beloved dogs. This particular bull terrier only had three
legs, and was a very bad tempered animal indeed. For me it
was an object of great hatred. One morning as I walked down
to breakfast, it flew at me, and had every intention of latching
on to my shin. I am afraid I kicked out at it, and catching it
on the half volley, sent it spinning about thirty yards down the
corridor along the parquet flooring. Unfortunately for me,
Susie saw this episode as she came out of a doorway. I had
been hoping to go out shooting that morning with the rest of
the party, but instead she sent me in to Stirling to order some
underfelt, sufficient to cover the whole of this shiny downstairs corridor. I met up with the shooters at lunch time, having accomplished my mission in the town. 'How much will
the underfelt be?' Susie asked. 'Seventy six pounds.' 'Well,'
she said, 'I don't think that's too bad, do you?'

'It's about seventy five pounds and ninety pence more than
a .22 bullet.' I replied. This was not a clever remark, and we
never really saw eye to eye afterwards.

General Wheeler became a great friend, and looked after
me as if he was my father. He was a superb officer, and he did
not suffer fools gladly, but he certainly understood that young
people sometimes make mistakes, and by and large he was
magnanimous in his forgiveness. This was stretched to break-
ing point on several occasions. One weekend I went, with
Charlie Enderby and Geoffrey van Cutsem, to the north coast
of Germany, where we had heard there was some marvellous

duck shooting to be had. We arrived at our estuary just before dark, and were settling ourselves down to prepare for the flight of duck and geese when we realised we were not alone, because we could hear movements in the undergrowth all around us. Seconds later, half a dozen Dutch policemen swooped onto our hides and ordered us to go with them. It transpired that our map reading was flawed, and we were in fact just in Holland, not in Germany as we had thought and we had ended up in a bird sanctuary, where, obviously, no shooting was allowed. We were taken in a van to the police station where we were thrown into the cells, and locked up individually for the night. Our guns were confiscated, and in fact, when Geoffrey finally got his back, it had been damaged so badly that it was never usable again. Next morning I was allowed one telephone call, so I rang my boss, the General. Initially he was very annoyed, but he soon understood that the three of us were in a serious predicament. To my surprise, he said he would send a car to collect us, providing he could persuade the Dutch authorities to release us without charge. This duly happened, and I was eternally grateful to him, particularly as the distance the staff car had to travel was nearly two hundred miles in each direction.

CHAPTER 8

HOW NOT TO BEHAVE
WHEN A HOUSE GUEST

MY LAST POSTING in the seven years I was in the Army was to Bovington near Wareham in Dorset, as an instructor at the Junior Leaders Regiment. I had already told my superiors that I was going to leave the Army, to pursue a career in the City, so to be stationed in England for the year prior to my departure was a great bonus. Party time!

During the previous couple of years I had become friendly with Stoker Hartington, and on my return from Germany he kindly asked me to shoot pheasants at Chatsworth during the last weekend in January. This was a lovely invitation and I arrived on the Thursday evening with my golden retriever, Kelpie, in good time for dinner. Chatsworth is a truly remarkable house in which to be a guest. I was shown to my bedroom, the Red Velvet, which was on the first floor close to the main drawing room (and the drink tray on a very large round table). We had an extremely late night that first evening, and I am afraid what with all the excitement I must have over-imbibed. Anyway, I was about to go to bed when I remembered that poor Kelpie was still sitting in the back of my car. I had not asked permission to bring her into the house, but it was an incredibly cold night, so I decided to go downstairs and sneak her up into my bedroom. All went well, and I fell on my bed at about three in the morning, with Kelpie lying at its foot. About an hour later, I was woken from my slumber by the unmistakable noise of a dog about to be very sick indeed. 'My God, the Aubusson!' I thought. Forgetting I was naked, I shot up off the bed and grabbed poor Kelpie by the muzzle. I opened the door and propelled her along the passage towards the drawing room. There I threw open the door, ran with her across the room, and opened the large French windows which give on to some steps down into the garden. There I released the unwitting dog, by this time half suffocating in her own sick. I let her wander around for a few minutes, but as I mentioned, it was an unbelievably cold night and I realised my body was shaking violently. I called Kelpie and we ran back up the steps, closed the French windows, and returned to the warmth of the four-poster in the Red Velvet Bedroom. The next morning I went downstairs for breakfast, at about nine o'clock and feeling slightly the worse for wear. It was being served in a large room in the basement called the Bachelor Parlour. As soon as I went through the door, everyone started laughing. Since I had told no one about the episode with my lovely dog, I couldn't initially imagine what was causing such merriment, until it transpired that the duty Security Officer had shown Stoker a film clip of me (in my birthday suit) dragging my retriever along the passage, and then – looking even less manly after five minutes in the freezing night air – returning to my bedroom. Stoker had thought fit to show this to the other guests just before I came in to breakfast.

I forgot to thank the Head Keeper at the end of the shooting day, so during tea I asked the Duchess of Devonshire

79

where I could find him. 'Oh, he'll be in the gunroom cleaning the guns.' 'How do I get to the gunroom?' Long pause. 'Do you know, I haven't the faintest idea,' she said.

Debo Devonshire is a fund of anecdotes, and has an incredible memory for humorous moments. She once told me that soon after her arrival at Chatsworth, in 1952, she was summoned by the Head Keeper to his house at eleven o'clock one morning. Amazingly, Mr Maclaughlan had been in charge since 1905. He was unable to drive, so he had been provided with his own chauffeur, and was a major force to be reckoned with. (His brother was the Station Master at Liverpool Street Station.) Debo was ushered into the parlour by one of his three spinster daughters, and kept waiting by the great man for twenty minutes. When he finally appeared, the interview was very short. 'Your Grace,' he said, 'I've asked you here today, to let you know that you may go wherever you want on the Estate.' End of meeting.

Surprisingly, the episode with my poor dog did not do me any lasting damage in the eyes of Stoker's parents, and on June 21st 1965 I was one of the guests staying at Chatsworth for his 21st birthday dance. This was a phenomenal occasion, with six hundred and fifty guests, many of whom arrived on a private train from London. Stoker's great uncle, Harold Macmillan, was staying in the house along with thirty-three others, and the whole coming-of-age celebrations lasted for three days. The dance itself was held in the Great Dining Room with supper served by candlelight in the Sculpture Gallery.

During this fabulous night, I murmured to a friend of mine 'With all these amazing pictures, surely they wouldn't miss this little one?' – at which point I took a very small Dutch Old Master off the wall as a joke, and then replaced it immediately. About two minutes later I felt a large hand on my shoulder, and a security guard asked me what I thought I was doing pulling one of the pictures down. Had I in fact intended to steal it? I reassured him, and said that I really had meant no harm, and I begged him not to write anything in his report. I was terrified in case the Duke got to hear about it. He assured me that he would say nothing. There was a splendid cricket match the next day with some of Stoker's friends taking on a team drawn from employees of the estate. At the end of the match the cup was presented to our winning team by the Duke. He said 'Many congratulations to you; please keep this silver trophy a long way from Nick Peto, because last night he tried to take one of my pictures from the drawing room, and I imagine he would like to have this in his suitcase as well!' Of course it was said with 'tongue in cheek'; Andrew Devonshire was a tremendous ally of mine over the years, and I always valued his good friendship and advice enormously. Prior to the cricket match, many of us went to a church service in Edensor. Stoker read the lesson, St John Ch. 20, and made only one serious slip, saying '... and they saw two angels in whites.' This brought a smile to many of the congregation.

That August, Henry Lopes invited me for a week's fishing on his father's river in Sutherland. I had been three or four times before; the first occasion was when Henry and I were still at Cothill in 1949, the year his father, Lord Roborough, bought the estate near Bettyhill, and two beats on the river Naver. I accepted immediately, since all my previous journeys to

Skelpick Lodge had been tremendous fun. Although Henry was twenty-six in 1965, the same age as me, he was still in awe of both his mother and father. The lunch pack we used to be given before going stalking or fishing was completely inedible, normally consisting of a very tired scotch egg, a badly bruised apple, and a flask of water. This assortment was placed in a Second World War gas mask holder, and the whole thing was a most unappetising prospect, even for hungry lads. On the third morning I suggested to Henry that we went to the Bettyhill Hotel, where I would buy some decent sandwiches for both of us and a bottle of wine. This we did, and after an uneventful morning's fishing we decided to have our lunch. I opened the wine, which was nicely chilled, having been sunk in the river and I was just about to take my first sip when to my amazement Henry grabbed the bottle and threw it into the middle of the water. I couldn't believe what he had done, and I was about to remonstrate with him when he showed me, in the far distance, the figure of his father coming up the river bank to see how we were getting on. I reminded him that I had paid for the wine so I couldn't believe that his father would mind, but Henry was not prepared to risk it.

There was a similar episode that evening. Lord Roborough always kept the key to the drinks cabinet in his pocket, so that the young could not help themselves to the spirits inside. The previous year Henry had had the foresight to take the key into the ironmonger in Bettyhill and have it copied. Lord and Lady Roborough went to bed at their usual time, about half past nine, saying (as always) that they hoped we would not stay down too long. As soon as they had disappeared Henry opened the cabinet and poured us both a large beaker of brandy. Henry was not one to dilute his drinks, preferring to take them neat. As Silas Weg says in *Our Mutual Friend*, 'He loved a gumtickler.'

We were standing against the fireplace warming ourselves in what was always an icy house, when we heard 'shuffle, shuffle, shuffle' coming back down the stairs. Henry said 'My God, I think that's Papa.' At that moment the door opened, and Lord Roborough in his dressing gown, pyjamas and slippers, peered round. Henry panicked, and threw the contents of his glass into the fire. There was a tremendous explosion and flames shot up both our backsides. The old boy did not notice, and merely said 'Have either of you seen the book I was reading?' Despite being red hot and well singed, neither Henry nor I moved, and both said we had not seen his book – at which point he withdrew.

The following morning I was to go stalking, and the rain was tipping down. I was being taken out by a tremendous character called Willie Duncan, a fine fisherman and stalker, who had been attached to the Skelpick Estate for many years – his nickname was 'The Laird of the Strath'. After a long and fruitless day, Willie and I returned wet through to the bone. My bedroom and bathroom were next door to the gun room, in a wooden annexe attached to the main lodge. I hopped into a hot bath as quickly as I could to try and thaw out and was lying there in a doze, when there was the most enormous BANG. I jumped out of my bath, and saw a hole had been drilled through the mat. Forgetting that I was starkers, I rushed into the gun room to see if Willie was all right. There he was, deeply shaken; he had fired the rifle by mistake just as he had started to clean it. There was a strong smell of cordite, and smoke was everywhere. At that moment Thompson, the ancient one-legged butler (who had been Lord Roborough's soldier servant in the Greys during the war), came hopping down the passage. As usual, he was pretty drunk, and I think he thought he was back in battle. 'Any wounded, any wounded?', he kept shouting.

I was desperately worried as to how I was going to keep this saga quiet, because I thought Lord Roborough might sack Willie if he found out about it. It transpired that he was actually in the Lodge at the time, but, amazingly, he had heard nothing. Apparently he was upstairs having the mother and father of an argument with Lady Roborough about who should have the first bath, as the hot water didn't run to two.

Back at Bovington, life for instructors of the Junior Leaders was quite tough. Three times during the year that I was there I had to take a group of the young lads (aged between fifteen and seventeen) on Outward Bound courses to Towyn in North Wales. I was obviously supposed to set an example by showing leadership, which sometimes was none too easy. I disliked rock climbing, and yet I had to appear unfazed, even though inside I was terrified. Each morning we had to run with these boys for the mile which separated our camp from the sea. Regardless of the time of year we had to dash into the sea and, in army parlance 'effect a complete immersion'. We would then jog back and have breakfast. Our day might include canoeing, hill walking, map reading, mountaineering or tackling the local assault course. It is at times of pressure like this, that one really finds out about oneself.

There was a beautiful little river nearby, so one Saturday I decided to see if I could poach a sea trout or salmon out of it. It was a perfect summer's evening, and the birds were chattering away like water flowing in a pipe. I had taken a small trout rod with me from Bovington, and I set off upstream to look for a likely spot. After I had walked for a while, I came across a pool beneath a steep waterfall, and it was obvious that no fish could swim up beyond this point. I tried my luck, but never saw a movement either to my fly or to any other lure floating on the surface. I felt sure there must be a fish or two in this deep still pool, and so I returned the following night with a couple of thunderflashes and a biscuit tin. I filled the tin with pebbles, lit one of the thunder flashes and popped it into the tin – putting the lid on as quickly as I could. I threw the 'bomb' three or four yards in front of me and watched it sink slowly in the peaty water. Suddenly, there was a deep boom and a small tidal wave appeared from where I had last seen my tin. After that, nothing. I was scanning the surface of the water, (by now it was nearly dark), when suddenly, one after another, about eight sea trout rose to the surface. I put my net under the nearest one and pulled it ashore. It was a beautiful fresh fish of about four pounds. I believe the others were only dazed, because after a few minutes there was no sign of them, and I imagine they must have recovered. Anyway, I took my trophy back to our camp, and we had a splendid late night barbecue.

CHAPTER 9

A DEBT OF HONOUR

I HAD FOUND MYSELF a new and glorious girlfriend. She was blonde, and extremely well formed. Her name was Susie Barden – she was nicknamed by my friends 'Give me a hardon, Barden'. I used to drive to London about once a fortnight and take her out to dinner, and afterwards we would go dancing. Ours was a very happy, bubbly relationship, with no complications. She was as sweet as a ripe apple. My pals were very envious and circled her like bees around a honey pot.

One Saturday Susie came down to visit me at Bovington. We drove to Weymouth for dinner in a marvellous fish restaurant, and had several glasses of wine, after which I suggested that we went back to the Camp to have a swim in the new indoor swimming pool. When I tried the gate to the pool it was locked, so I went to the Guard Room and asked the young cadet in charge for the key. By now it was midnight. I did not turn the lights on; it would be more romantic swimming in the dark. Naked into the pool we went, and started splashing about, and then cuddling and kissing. We were like two goldfish making love in their bowl. I thought of Ella Fitzgerald singing 'goldfish in the privacy of bowls do it: let's do it, let's fall in love …'

After five minutes or so I was appalled when all the lights

were suddenly switched on – with Susie and me embracing in the shallow end for all to see. The vile young cadet on duty in the Guard Room had spread the word that Captain Peto and his girlfriend were going for a swim, with the result that three hundred Junior Leaders had climbed out of bed, and were now peering through the glass wall when the lights came on. The cadets did have the decency to turn the lights off again after a few minutes, and we beat a hasty retreat.

I thought it would be possible to smuggle Susie into my bedroom in the Officers' Mess, provided I moved her out early on Sunday morning, before she was discovered. We both fell into a deep sleep, only to be woken by my soldier servant at eight o'clock. He saw that I had someone with me, and for some unknown reason reported the fact to the Adjutant, Richard Head. He did some research, found out about our midnight swim and, instead of calling me into his office and giving me a well-deserved rocket, reported both misdemeanours to the Commanding Officer, an extremely unpleasant man in the Royal Tank Corps. On the Monday morning I was summoned to his office, and told that, as what I had done was so outrageous, I would be sent for disciplining by the Colonel. I was then put in a staff car and sent to Tidworth, where I had to see Colonel Julian Berry. He read the notes on my crimes, told me I had been a bloody fool and let the matter rest there. He also added quietly that young cavalry officers were expected to overcook things from time to time – but he wouldn't imagine that a Tank Corps Colonel would understand that. It was a stupid thing to have done, but the affair was blown out of all proportion. Susie was such a splendid, spirited girl that she merely laughed at the whole episode, and couldn't believe that the Army could take a frolic so seriously.

Living in the beautiful countryside of Dorset for a year was marvellous. I had a horse down there, and hunted frequently with the South Dorset. Local people, like Richard and Janey Mead were unbelievably kind, offering both stabling and accommodation to all of us young officers. We went away for most weekends during the summer, playing golf and cricket and going to dances. But in the winter months one could have no better fun than staying put in Dorset and enjoying the sporting life there.

My father had a gun in a pheasant shoot at Bowood, an estate near Calne and one Friday he kindly asked Jake Morley and me to go in his place. It was not a good shoot by any standards, and the day we went was particularly disappointing. There was a howling gale blowing and the owner of the shoot, Charlie Shelburne, decided to call a halt at about three o'clock on that bleak November afternoon. He was going to London, and it would suit him to get started early. Jake and I put our guns and dogs in the back of my car, and went off to have a quick cup of tea in the Bowood kitchen. When we came out, the wind was still about force eight and we set off for home. As we motored down the drive we noticed several groups of duck flighting into a pond in a wood a little way off to our right. 'Why don't we go and see if we can shoot a few of those? That would liven up a dull day, and Charlie will be none the wiser,' I said.

We got our guns out, and nipped across the field to the flight pond where we found two immaculate hides, and were soon shooting away happily in the gloaming. After we had been at it for about fifteen minutes I was startled by a roar from just behind me. To my horror, there was Charlie, extremely angry (he had forgotten his briefcase). It transpired that this pond had been prepared for the following evening, when he had invited some grandee to come and flight duck with him.

Although I was taking Susie Barden out throughout 1965, I did also see one or two other girls. Simon Keswick had telephoned me from where he worked in Hong Kong and asked me to look after his girlfriend Yvonne while she was in London for a month on a modelling contract. He said she had nowhere to live in London, and asked me if I would have her to stay. I met Yvonne at Heathrow and couldn't believe how beautiful she was, tall, with an amazing figure and long jet black hair. That first evening, she and I went to a party given by a friend of mine, and we had a great time together, so that when we got back to my flat I thought it might be in order to look into her bedroom to say goodnight. I gave her a kiss, which seemed well received, so I suggested that I hopped in with her; at which point her little hand flew out from the bedclothes and hit me firmly two or three times across the cheek. 'I am Simon's friend,' she said, 'please don't ever forget it.' I went back to my room somewhat chastened, and fell asleep. About twenty minutes later I was woken by the door opening slowly, and this wonderful girl slipped quietly into my bed.

Yvonne stayed with me for a month, and I have never been exposed to such incredible femininity before or since. Every evening when I came back from work the whole flat would smell of incense, a hot bath would have been run, and

Yvonne would be there to pander to my every whim. In due course, she had to move on to New York. I was sad to see her go.

Many times in my life I have been mistaken for The Duke of Kent. Possibly the most embarrassing of these confrontations took place at the opening of Angela Nevill's new art gallery, when an old boy I knew slightly, Reggie Winn, came up to me and bobbed down his head. 'Hello, Sir,' he started, 'How was Canada?' I didn't want to confuse him by stating that I wasn't who he thought I was – so I said, 'Canada was great.' To my horror, Reggie replied, 'Let's go and sit down, Sir. I want to hear all about it. I did exactly the same trip as you way back in 1931.' I was about to run for it, when a friend came up, put his arm round my shoulders, and said, 'Hello, Reggie; I hope Nick's not pretending to be The Duke of Kent again?' Reggie Winn looked me up and down. 'My God, you're an imposter! This is completely unacceptable.' I didn't know where to put myself.

Twenty-five years after Susie Barden and I had our fling, and not having seen each other in the interim, I spotted her at a dance in London. I rushed up to say hello, but Susie looked bemused. 'I've just given you a huge hug and my best kiss,' she said. At that moment The Duke of Kent came by. 'I have heard it said that we look alike,' he murmured, 'but I never realised there would be any fringe benefits.'

For a brief moment around that time, I had another girl-friend, who had a lovely face, but who was rather large from the hips downwards. I nicknamed her 'the lobster', (all the meat is in the tail.) She was a great enthusiast, and for a moment I contemplated settling down with her, but luckily, after we had gone out together five or six times, she asked me to stay with her mother. Mum had a face like a sucked lemon, and was about as sour and I could envisage that my friend might well end up like her; I also think she would have pecked me to death. She was undeniably attractive, but I realised also that she was a picture of intellectual poverty. I beat a hasty retreat.

Towards the end of my time in the Army and in the months following, I became addicted to gambling. The game I really enjoyed playing was chemin de fer. I used to go one or two nights a week to the Clermont Club, a very plush set-up run by John Aspinall who used to encourage young men to play there, and enjoy themselves in the lap of luxury. He would give us free dinners, free drink, and generally make us feel pretty important. I had very little money, and so I started slowly. Sadly for me, after a short while I hit a tremendous winning streak – coming away with a cheque on thirteen consecutive visits. My winnings were between three hundred and two thousand pounds per night. I really thought I had cracked it.

I decided to celebrate my impending departure from the Army, and my new-found wealth by renting a house in the South of France. I took down there Susie Barden, Michael Pearson and some other friends – and I also asked my parents for a week. My father was bemused as to how I could have paid for such a lavish villa, equipped with a lovely swimming pool, a tennis court, and a speed boat in the harbour at Antibes, and he told me that in his day in the

Army there was no way that a Captain's salary would have stretched to all this. However had I managed to supplement my earnings? The last thing I wanted was for him to know that I had become a gambler, so I said that I had saved up money for the previous two years in order to have this holiday of a lifetime.

When I returned from France, having blown most of my ill-gotten cash, I decided to go and replenish the larder at the Clermont Club. I had dinner with Michael Pearson, after which we went upstairs to the 'chemmie' room. I shall never forget the next quarter of an hour as long as I live. The first 'shoe' of the evening was about to start. Ian Maxwell-Scott was at number one of the nine seats, Aspinall at number two; I sat down at number five, and Michael was next to me. Ian flicked a card into the middle of the table, and started the 'bank' with £100. 'Banco,' I said. The card was placed in front of me by the croupier. Then I received the second card. Between them they added up to six. Maxwell-Scott threw open his two cards, and he had seven. Oh dear, I thought, pushing a chip with £100 on it in his direction. I called 'suivi'. This meant that I would go against his bank again, but this time for £200 – his original £100, plus the £100 I had just lost. I lost again, and parted with a £200 chip. Ian ran that bank nine times, without garaging any of the profit. I followed each time, and in the space of a few ghastly minutes found myself losing £25,000.

'That will do me,' said Ian, about to pass the bank, and gather in the money. 'Let me have one more go at you,' I pleaded. I couldn't believe I could lose *ten* hands in succession: 'Are you good for the money?' interjected Aspinall. 'You know I am,' I lied. 'O.K. then,' said Ian, 'this is my last hand; if I win I shall pass the bank.'

The first card was flicked over to me. A king – worth nought. Ian dealt one for himself, but did not look at it; it remained face down. My second card came over. I put my two cards together, and very slowly examined the newcomer. An eight! Virtually perfect. I placed my cards face up and said 'peut être'. Ian picked up his two cards, gently prising them apart.

'I am so sorry, old fellow,' he said, 'mais j'ai neuf – Napoleon.' Nine was unbeatable, and he had done me. I had lost fifty grand in the blink of an eye.

I felt the bottom fall out of my life. I went to the 'Caisse', and told the head croupier, Monsieur Marianni, that I would settle up in the morning. I went outside into the starlit world of Berkeley Square, and started walking, my head about to burst as the enormity of my folly began to sink in. I knew I could not tell my father; I also knew I could not begin to pay. I thought I would walk down to the Embankment and sit on a bench until I summoned up courage to jump into the swirling, muddy, moonlit river.

As I wandered along, head down, a desperate sight, I felt a hand come gently down on my shoulder. I looked up, and found my old ally Andrew Parker Bowles. 'You look dreadful,' he said.

'I am. I can't begin to describe to you what an ass I've been.'

'Don't tell me anything,' he said. 'My car's right here. Hop in, and you can stay the night with me. Tell me your story tommorrow, and we'll make a plan.'

93

What a good friend. I got in his car, shaking like a leaf, and off we went. The next morning, I described what had happened, and Andrew's jaw dropped further and further. 'You have to bite the bullet, and tell your father,' he said, after much deliberation. So I did.

As gambling debts could not be legally enforced, I suggested to my father that maybe I simply did not need to pay. He was appalled, and thundered that this loss was a debt of honour and must of course be paid in full. I had a Trust Fund which had in it just enough money. In due course this was broken, my debts were paid to Aspinall, and the fund was then wound up.

For many years after this sorry episode I pottered back to various casinos in London. Like all gamblers I desperately wanted to recoup my losses. For a while I became a 'house player' at the White Elephant in Curzon Street for the proprietor, Tony Mancini. This was hard graft. I had to play poker all night until the last people departed, which was normally about four o'clock. I was allowed to keep twenty five per cent of my winnings, but if I lost, that would be put on the slate also. Of course in the morning I had to go off as normal to my job. Mancini was a very tough cookie, and I dread to think what would have happened if for any reason I had let him down.

Looking back, I don't have too many regrets about my gambling, although undoubtedly I was an overall loser. But it was exciting, and on the few occasions when I did have a large amount of cash in my pocket it was fun to take friends out to dinner – or indeed, to the South of France.

*

I stayed with Andrew in the Portobello Road for about six months. His only rule was that I was on no account to use his bedroom – the largest room in this tiny, but very pretty house. I had to sleep in the spare room, which was minute, with only a small single bed and a chair. At the White Elephant, I had met a gamblerholic called Katarina Zitko. A large Yugoslavian woman, she had been a professional swimmer in her youth, and once told me that she had escaped from her parents and her village, by swimming from Yugoslavia to Italy.

One morning I took her to lunch at the Mirabelle. She had a voracious appetite, and devoured no less than two and a half dozen oysters, as well as a bottle of Dom Perignon. I reckoned after this gastronomic experience she would surely be hot to trot, so I rushed her back to Portobello. Andrew was with his Regiment in Germany, so I thought nothing of slipping into his bedroom that afternoon. Katarina undressed and laid her large, but muscular body on the bed. She complained of feeling unwell, and shut her eyes; the room was beginning to spin, she said. As I was about to climb on board, the telephone rang. It was Andrew.

'You picked the telephone up far too quickly,' he said. 'You must be in my bedroom.'

'I was doing some dusting,'

'Well I hope that's true, because I'm in a taxi with my girl-friend, and I'm on my way from Heathrow to Portobello. I'll be there in fifteen minutes. Make yourself scarce.'

Panic stations! Miss Zitko had fallen into a drunken stupor, and I had to smack her a little to wake her. She sat bolt upright in Andrew's bed, and I saw at once that she was going to be sick.

I bundled Katarina down the narrow staircase towards the bathroom on the half landing. But too late. Andrew had photographs of himself all the way down the stairs: Me on *The Fossa* completing the Grand National; Me with my E-type Jaguar; Me winning the army 100 yards. That sort of thing. Every one of these pictures was hit by one of Katarina's oysters – they were propelled everywhere. Having shoved her into the bathroom, I grabbed a towel, and desperately began to mop up. The girl reappeared, a little less dishevelled, and I told her to get into her clothes and leave. Time was hurtling by. Katarina went out of the door, and I reckoned I had only five minutes before Andrew arrived. I smoothed the bed, had a last tidy up on the staircase, and ran down to the hall. The bath towel I had been using was now extremely potent and unpleasant. Where could I hide it? In desperation, I saw a little door under the stairs. I opened this and pushed the towel onto the slatted shelf at the top. I dashed out of the door, and raced to my car. Andrew and his girlfriend were walking towards me, about fifty yards away. I hopped in, and put my head between my knees. Moments later, they walked past, and I peeped out just in time to see them go through his front door.

I drove back to my office, exhausted, but confident that I had got away with it. The telephone on my desk rang. 'I don't know what on earth you have been up to here, but there is a really foul smell,' Andrew said. 'My friend has left as she was so nauseous. What have you done?'

'I don't know what you're talking about, Andy.' He rang off, and I went back to work. About an hour later he called again. 'The smell is now so horrendous, I am going to have to move out myself – please, please tell me what you did.' So I told Andrew about the towel full of oysters, and where I had hidden it. 'Oh, no!' he screamed, 'You've put it on top of the hot water cistern. No wonder these fumes are wafting through the floorboards and into my bedroom. You're fired – don't bother coming back, except to collect your clothes.' Not good, I'm afraid – and Andrew had been such a phenomenally staunch ally to me in my hour of need.

Katarina was altogether too much for me, so I introduced her to Rid Morgan Jones, a very old friend and a renowned swordsman. She thought he was a far better bet than me in every way, and they sailed off into the sunset together – greatly to my relief.

CHAPTER 10

THE YELLOW BIRD

AND SO I LEFT the Army, and set about trying to find a job in the City to make my fortune. But Civvy Street was no push over; I was now twenty-seven, and without qualifications. I talked things through with a good friend, Rupert Hambro who told me that Hambros Bank owned a Commodity Brokers called G W Joynson and Co, and he suggested that I applied for an interview with Colin Joynson, the Chairman. I did so and was accepted into the firm as a humble clerk in the Accounts Department. No doubt Rupert had put in a good word for me. My salary was to be five hundred and fifty pounds per year, and the plan was for me to spend two or three months in each department learning the ropes. They did not want me to join them until early in the new year (1967), so I looked forward to two months holiday, probably the last large chunk of free time for many years to come.

I was very pushed for cash that autumn, but one thing I did have left from my gambling spree was a good colt called *Sharp Work*, which was in training with Ginger Dennistoun. I had won some money off him in one of the innumerable poker games we played at that time, and he offered me the two-year-old in lieu of his debt. *Sharp Work* won his first two races, and then was second in the next two. By this stage Lester Piggott had taken an interest, and he asked if he could ride him in the Park Lodge Nursery at Newmarket towards the end of August. We were a short priced favourite, but I backed the colt as if there was no tomorrow. Lester rode a beautiful race, cruising up through the last furlong and winning by three quarters of a length. *Sharp Work* was then sold, for eight thousand pounds, enormously helping my bank balance.

That winter I went skiing in St Moritz. This was only my second effort on skis, and the pals I went with were far more proficient. I remember losing control down the nursery slope, and only coming to a halt when my skis went through the side window of a Volkswagen parked on the sunken road at the bottom. I was out there for ten days, and took a guide for the mornings, so that in the end I could manage most runs, albeit slowly.

My friends were beginning to get married. Archie Stirling had married Charmian Scott and Charlie Hornby married Amanda Hyde, Willy Bulwer-Long had married Sarah Rawlinson and Chips Keswick had married Sarah Ramsay. Rupert Lycett Green and Candida Betjeman had embarked on a marriage which has now spanned over forty years and proved immensely happy. Indeed, all these marriages lasted the course, with the exception of Archie and Charmian. Archie's second wife was the incomparable actress, Diana Rigg (deservedly a Dame, for services to the theatre). I began to wonder if it was time for me to settle down.

As a final fling before I went to work at G W Joynson, I decided to accept an invitation from my old friend Charles Spencer-Churchill to go and stay in his father's house near Montego Bay, in Jamaica. The other house guests were Jake and Kirsty Morley, Christina Shand Kydd, Simon and Andrew Parker Bowles and Camilla Shand. It was the time

when Flower Power was the vogue, and we were pho-
tographed in the swimming pool as flower children for an
American glossy magazine. We looked ridiculous.

One night we went clubbing in Montego Bay, and ended
up in a seedy place called the Yellow Bird. I became enam-
oured of a local girl, and had several dances with her. At that
point Charles told me everyone was going home, and if I
wanted a lift I must leave with them, but my lady had asked
me to go to her house for a night cap, which sounded far more
appealing, so I told Charles that I would find my own way
back later on. The girl and I got into a taxi and were driven
for about two miles through the poorer part of Montego Bay,
up into the hills. It wasn't until the cab stopped outside a ram-
shackle corrugated-roofed building that I realised I could be
in big trouble.

This was the first real brothel I had ever visited, and I
began to sober up quickly. I went upstairs with the girl, to a
cubicle which was only divided from the next one by a thin
piece of plywood. The grey, striped mattress (there were no
sheets) was covered with old cigarette burns, and a naked light
bulb swung dimly from the ceiling. I gave the girl such money
as I had, and told her that, after all, I didn't feel like taking
things further. I shot down the stairs, only to be met at the
bottom by a large black man who told me that I was not to
insult one of his 'daughters' by running out on her, and to
return and finish the job. Terrified, I whizzed upstairs, leapt
on top of the lady for a couple of minutes and then ran down
into the street. By this stage it was dawn, and I had at least five
miles to negotiate between the brothel and home.

I wandered back towards Montego Bay along the shingle

track that the taxi had come down earlier, trying to thumb a lift; the road was empty. But, as I entered the outskirts of the town, I saw a large Cadillac coming up behind me, so I flagged it down and begged a ride. I told the burly American driver that I needed to go a couple of miles the other side of Montego Bay; he said that was fine because he was on his way to Round Hill, so I jumped in and began to relax in the passenger seat. 'You're just who I wanted to see,' I said to him. To my horror, he put his hand on my thigh and said, 'And you're just who I wanted to see.' I was petrified. I told him that I had had a very busy evening already, and that with the best will in the world, I had nothing left to offer. He drove me past our front gates and stopped the car. I opened the passenger door and flew out, followed a few yards behind by this enormous fellow. He ran after me across the croquet lawn, but I was quicker than him, and reached the sanctuary of the house with a second to spare.

I decided not to tell anyone about this ghastly episode, and came down to breakfast at about nine o'clock in the normal way. Everyone else was already at the table and I was about to help myself to some cornflakes and fruit, when the Jamaican butler, Malcolm, came in to the dining room and started chortling loudly.

'What on earth are you laughing at?' demanded Charles.

'Oh Man,' Malcolm said, looking at me, 'if you'd tripped over one of them croquet hoops, that fella would have split you in two!'

So, much to my chagrin, the story was out, and I was the laughing stock of the party. Malcolm had been watering the roses, and had enjoyed a ringside view of the whole saga.

CHAPTER 11

THE ROCKY DOCKY
SHOW

THUS MY HOLIDAYS came to an end, and it was time to settle down and go to work in an office, for the first time in my life. I went off to Truefitt and Hill to have my hair cut by my good friend Mr Christopher. He carried out this menial task for over forty years of my life, and I always looked forward to my time in his chair. He is a Cypriot, mad on racing, and loved to chat up the manicurists. One of the better remarks he and I overheard was when an old boy with a hearing aid in the next door chair was having his manicure from a very attractive young lady, her leg between his thighs. She smiled at him and said, 'Excuse me, m' Lord, would you like your cuticles pushed back?'

To which he replied, 'I think if you move your knee, they'll go back on their own.'

From there I went to see my friend Rupert Lycett Green, in his new venture, Blades the Tailors in Savile Row. I ordered two dark suits, and one rather more dashing pale grey number – all on the 'never never'. Now I was all set. On the first morning that I arrived at 52 Cornhill I realised that I needn't have bothered with my clothing. I was ushered into the back office and put under the wing of the senior accountant, whom I will call 'Ray Small'. My job was writing out contracts of clients' trades in longhand, and working out their profit and loss and our commission. After only a month or so it became apparent to me that Mr Small was on the fiddle. I paid more attention from then on, and it seemed that he was in cahoots with one of our larger clients. This posed a difficult question for me; should I go to Colin Joynson and tell him what I suspected? If my suspicions then proved groundless I would probably lose my job. I could not pin down exactly how money was being syphoned off, so I always had a nagging feeling that I might be imagining things. In the end, about three months after I started there, I did see Mr Joynson and told him in confidence what I thought was going on. Nothing happened for a further month, and I began to think that I must have been mistaken, and perhaps had misjudged Ray Small. However, one morning, when I walked into our little office, neither he nor the assistant next to him were there. I was told they would not be coming back, and that the only two remaining people, which included me, would now have to run the back office on our own until another accountant was found. Apparently, the two men had relieved G W Joynson and Co of nearly two hundred thousand pounds during the previous eighteen months.

A day or two later Rupert telephoned me in the office to say that he had just been made a member of White's, and would I like to lunch with him? I hightailed it from Cornhill to St James's Street, and met him on the steps of the Club punctually at 12.30. He was wearing one of his newest creations, an avocado coloured suit with red braiding. We went to the bar together, and the only other people there were two old boys sitting on the bench nearby. Before Rupert even had time to order us a drink, one of them let out a tremendous 'Umph'.

'My God, I think I just saw a man in a green suit, Maurice!' he said to the barman, 'is there a visiting Club this month – maybe it's the AA or the RAC, or perhaps the Turf Club?'

Rupert, completely unabashed, turned round and eyeballed the old member still sitting on his perch, and said, 'I think you must be referring to me, sir. You might be interested to know that I am not a member of the AA or the RAC, and I was recently blackballed for the Turf Club – but I am a member of Whites.'

'Good Lord young man, I wasn't talking about *you*. You look absolutely splendid,' said the old member.

My pal Jake Morley approached me one day over lunch and asked if I would like to join him and his colleague Michael Doxford; they had a commodity broking business, and were keen to move from the City to the West End. After some negotiation it was decided that they would link up with Joynsons, and that the three of us would open an office in Hamilton Place, off Park Lane – but still be part of the Joynson Group.

After we had been in our new office for a short while, we did in fact leave the original company to form our own business, M L Doxford & Co. This was a very exciting adventure; Michael was the largest shareholder, with Jake and myself having sixteen per cent each. Michael was Chairman and Jake was Managing Director. We furnished our office, 140 Piccadilly, with three impressive desks, and had a large reception area. On the wall was a huge plastic board, on which all the commodity prices were posted, two or three times a day. We found ourselves two attractive secretaries, an Australian called Annabelle and Clare, a lovely South African girl. In order for the prices at the top of the board to be changed, one or other of them had to climb a step ladder and reach up as high as she could with her left hand, which always caused merriment, because in the days of the mini skirt there was not much left to our imaginations from where we sat behind our desks. In the grip of a hangover one morning, Michael said to Annabelle, 'I'll tell you what I'll do. If you stop wearing knickers I'll increase your pay by a £1 a day.' She laughed, but continued to arrive in all her underwear, smiling provocatively. In 1973 she left us and was replaced by Miranda Sellers, recently divorced from her husband Peter whom she had married in 1969. Miranda would arrive looking a million dollars, despite the early hour, and her two Pekingese came with her, passing the day on a large cushion by her desk.

Things went well for us at the outset, and our office became ever busier, with all types of affluent clients calling by to trade in such things as gold, cocoa, copper, sugar and the like. From 1970 to 1975 we had a tremendous run – that is to say our clients did extremely well – and the positions we took in the markets for our Company were also successful; this led to some excesses. Michael Doxford became a powerboat enthusiast, and broke some records with his two main vehicles, Limit Up and Limit Down: Jake was enormously involved in National Hunt Racing and owned several good horses, all of which were trained by his brother David. We used to have long and very good lunches at various watering holes in the West End. *Les Ambassadeurs* was just across the road from the office; we would also go to Wilton's, and afterwards play endless games of £1 note poker with Mr Marks, the Manager. 1973 was a year of major depression in the Stock Market, and we were fortunate to have a great deal of money in our company's bank account. Michael was a fantastic entrepreneur, always on the look-out for new opportunities. It was not until a few years later that the business began to wobble and earned its nickname, The Rocky Docky Show.

One day in early 1974, when the FTSE 100 Index was sinking by several per cent each day (to a low of 170), he came into the office and said that he thought we ought to bid for The Ritz which had just come on the market. We had enjoyed a fantastic run in commodities, a notoriously fickle business, and if we could get into the hotel trade it would be a much safer platform for the future. We did in fact bid three and a half million pounds for the *Ritz*, but were not successful. A company called Trafalgar House bought the hotel with a bid only slightly larger than ours. Had we made this transition, life would certainly have been very different. But our office continued to be a popular venue, and was never dull. Lord Lucan used to call in every morning at midday, and have a Martini (or two) on his way to the Clermont for lunch.

It was John Lucan who taught me one of my favourite limericks.

'I love a Martini,' said Mabel,
But I only have one at the most,
'Cos two and I'm under the table,
And three, I'm under my host!'

One of our younger clients, just beginning to make his way in the property world, told me the following story. He had gone to The Mirabelle to entertain his bank manager and on his arrival in that lovely restaurant, he spotted Sir Charles Clore having lunch with a friend. Sir Charles had made a vast fortune in property and Sears Holdings, which included Selfridges and Saxone shoes – anything he touched seemed to turn to gold.

Our young hero, who had only once met the great man, went boldly up and introduced himself. 'I know you like helping young people, Sir Charles. Can I ask you a big favour? When you leave you will pass my table. Will you acknowledge me in a very friendly way? This will impress my lunch guest enormously.' '

Of course I will,' said Clore with a smile.

In due time he came past the young man's table.

'Hello, Anthony – very good to see you,' beamed Sir Charles.

'Oh, bugger off Charlie: Can't you see I'm busy?' came the reply.

But I must backtrack for a moment. At the end of 1968, I had fallen in love with the most wonderful American girl. Anne Tysen was working on the editorial staff of *Vogue* magazine, and I had met her at the wedding of a mutual friend, Oliver Baring. Oliver telephoned me just before the big day and said that two beautiful American girls were coming over, and one of them was the daughter of one of the richest men in the world, so I should cast my eye carefully over her. After the wedding I pursued Anne to Paris, and in due course rang

Oliver to tell him so and that things were going very well; I was about to go down on bended knee. There was a pause on the other end of the telephone, and then Oliver said, 'Oh bother, I think you've gone after the wrong one!'

'Why so?' said I.

'Well,' he said, 'Susan Engelhard is in Australia, and she was the girl I was talking about. The one you are chasing, Anne Tysen, is a heavenly girl but she has no cash.'

'Oh dear, Oliver' I said, 'I thought she was called Anne Thyssen.'

But by this stage I was head-over-heels in love with Anne, and we got married in New York on April 11th 1969. We had an amazing honeymoon in Jamaica for ten days, and then went on a yacht we had been lent by Sarah Roubanis at Key Largo. We were meant to be there for four days, but the Captain turned out to be an alcoholic, which was disappointing in the extreme. On our first night I caught him leering through our bedroom porthole, mouthing 'Go on my son …' which was hopelessly offputting.

When we returned to England I bought a two-bedroomed flat in Walpole Street, where we started our married life. Anne was given a splendid pure white pekingese, by her great friend and fellow American, Robin Hambro; we called the dog 'Milkshake', and she would take her off to work at *Vogue* each morning in the basket of her bicycle.

We would often stay in London at weekends, but, if an invitation came to go to the country we were happy to do that as well. It was in November 1969 that Neil and Serena McConnell invited us, for the first time, to shoot in Czechoslovakia, a truly amazing adventure, which was repeated in both the two following years. We were flown in a private aeroplane to Vienna, and stayed the first night with Neil's step-father in Schloss Enzesfeld. Nothing was spared. We changed into dinner jackets every evening; Serena had brought a hair stylist on the aeroplane for the girls, and caviare was the norm before dinner. Neil had hired a fleet of Mercedes to take the twenty or so members of the party across the border to Zidlochovice, which was near the town of Brno (where the Bren gun was invented). This castle used to be the hunting palace of the last Austrian Emperor, Franz Joseph and had remained in a time warp for the past fifty-five years; many aspects were completely unchanged since before the First World War. There were stuffed animals everywhere, and dusty eagles swinging gently in the breeze, from wires in the high ceilings. The dining room had literally hundreds of antlers around the walls, with a vast horn chandelier over the middle of the table.

One of our fellow guests was my most favourite girl (sadly, never a girlfriend in the true sense) called Chubby Gerard Leigh. One night, two of us manoeuvred one of the stuffed bears into her bed, with its head on her pillows. We placed a stag's hoof upright between its loins, and pulled up the bed-clothes. When Chubby came out of her bathroom, before hopping into bed, she sat at her dressing table, and carefully put some curlers into her hair. We had the door ajar, and five of us could see her on the little stool, meticulously going through her nightly routine. She finally stood up, switched off the dressing table lights, and turned towards her huge four-poster bed. Seconds later, the scream she let out must have woken half of Czechoslovakia.

We would leave the Palace by six-thirty each morning, and drive straight to the shooting grounds. After a couple of pheasant drives, a spectacular brunch was laid out on tables in a clearing in one of the woods – linen table cloths, cut glass, silver cutlery, everything had found its way out there for our feast. Much vodka was drunk, and then after an hour or so, shooting resumed. We were under instructions only to shoot cock pheasants, and although a few mistakes were made, basically, the bag did comprise only cocks. There were about two hundred beaters and forty keepers, many of whom would have been the foresters. Each gun had two loaders, mostly ancient retainers, and not particularly adept at this task. The first year we went, one of the men looking after me spoke a little English, and he could well remember the Emperor shooting pheasants in the same area to which we went, back in 1910. Our bags were enormous, varying between two and three thousand head per day. In the evening all the game was laid out in immaculate straight lines, row upon row. Bonfires would be lit at each corner of the tableau and speeches would be made, with tunes from the hornblowers prior to each one. This was an integral part of the sport, steeped in tradition and performed in order to honour the dead animals, and the professionalism of all who had taken part. This shoot attracted some of the very best shots of that era, particularly Bill Stirling, with his son Archie, Sunny Marlborough, and François Riocour, who had recently won an Olympic skeet medal. Less good, but equally enthusiastic, was an Italian fellow called Anibile Scotti-Casanova (I think he added the Casanova himself). He spoke very little English, but at the end of each drive he would dance up to his neighbour and get out his one phrase: 'How many you get? I get sixty-five. I am swinging superbly and shooting impeccably.'

As we walked through the snow to the ponies and traps after the final drive of that first expedition, I said to Neil, 'You know, in England we would have to tip the keeper £5 per hundred pheasants.' 'Well,' said he, 'that's what I thought we'd do here.' I made a lightening calculation. In the three days, we had shot seven thousand birds – that would be £350. Nasty. I suggested to Neil that I go round the ten guns, and collect the money from them – and then he could present the Head Keeper with one large bundle. I reckoned I could leave my £350 out of the pile, and he would not notice. However, he saw me coming I think, and said that he would prefer it if we all thanked the keeper individually – so my pockets were plum empty as we set off for home.

Neil McConnell, (who sadly died many years ago), was a tremendously generous host. He was always renting shoots, and Annie and I were lucky enough to be asked to most of them. We went with him to Fenton, in Northumberland, a magical white house, set most beautifully in a large fir wood, not many miles from the sea. The estate is owned by Lord Lambton, himself a superb shot. One year, in the early 1970s, we were up there for the first time, and the weather was appalling. After breakfast, I came down to put on my wet weather gear. It was very dark indeed inside the house, although there was a blazing fire in the far corner of the hall. I saw Serena McConnell pulling on a pair of thigh-length white fur boots, with some difficulty. She was a very old friend, so I went up behind her and goosed her sharply in the bum. 'Typical you to wear such inappropriate kit,'

I said, 'you really have got no idea how to dress for this type of weather.' She was still facing away from me, but drew herself up to her full height, and slowly turned round. It was my host's wife, Bindy Lambton, whom I had never met before. She looked caustically at me, and said in front of everyone, 'I've no idea who you are, but I shall wear what I like, when I like, in my own house.' Many years later, I sat next to her at David Metcalfe's splendid 70th birthday dinner. I was at the end of the table, with no one on my right, so I concentrated hard on Bindy, and towards the end of the evening I really felt things had gone well. Just at that point she turned to me, and said, 'I was told by David Beaufort that you are a really amusing man. You are obviously having an off-day.' A bit disappointing, after all the effort I had put in.

The only problem I had with Neil's shoots was that mostly, he did invite very important people – myself excepted. Simon Gray, who managed Fenton and placed the guns, would always put people like Sunny Marlborough and Jamie Niven in the middle of the line. Slightly miffed at yet again being on the outside, I was travelling in the very back of Simon's long-wheelbase landrover (with all the swells in front), when I said to Jake Morley 'Jakie, you know this estate I've bought in Devon? It's just an investment really, and I'm never going to go there, so I have got to get someone to manage it for me. You don't by any chance know of anyone do you?' At which Jake said, 'Well that's a funny thing, I've just bought an estate in Cumbria, and it's fifteen thousand acres, but I too will need someone to look after it for me.' Simon heard this dialogue, and our ruse worked

Anne and Milkshake going to work at *Vogue*, 1972.

Derby Day, 1979. Standing from left to right: Michael Buckley, Candida Lycett Green, Anna Wallis, Dan Meinertzhagen, Lucinda Peto, NP, Sarah Davidson, Archie Stirling, Amabel Lindsay; seated from left to right: Michael White, Duncan Davidson, Rupert Lycett Green

'Milla Irwin and Andrew Parker Bowles, 1979 at Dean Manor.

My son, Alexander, on the Naver, 1981.

The Marchessini Dance, Syon House, June 1983. From left to right: Alexander (uncle of the girls), Atalanta, Lucinda, Tatiana, Demetri, Cassandra and Lucinda Peto, mother of the girls.

NP on Marble Arch at a meet of the Heythrop Hounds, Lower Slaughter, 1984.

On board *Albacorra*, October 1988. Top left: NP and Rupert Baring; top right: Suki Paravicini and NP; below: Maggie Heath, NP, Chubby Gerard Leigh and Oliver Baring.

Henry Lopes, 1989.

Teasel retrieving at Hutchen Gill, Bolton Abbey, 1989.

Nicholas Soames, grouse
shooting at Commonburn.

Zoë with Candida Lycett Green at Huish, near Marlborough, 1991.

Our wedding lunch, 19th December 1991. From left to right: Zoë, NP, Anne and Martin Summers, Rupert Lycett Green, Rhydian Morgan Jones, Camilla Parker Bowles.

Joy and Ronnie Barker with Zoë in our garden, 1992.

brilliantly. For the rest of the day Jake and I were right under the tap.

The big excitement in early 1970 was the musical *Hair*. It was a wonderful show, and caused much comment because at one stage several of the performers stripped off completely – an unheard of thing then. Annie and I went to see the show with Princess Anne, who was accompanied by 'a sandy-haired man in his late-twenties'. (*The Daily Telegraph* 20/2/70). It was Andrew Parker Bowles. Women have always fallen at his feet, and with good reason. He is attentive, intelligent and has enormous charm.

In November 1970 Anthony Speelman and his father, Edward, asked me whether I would like to go to an important Old Master sale at Christie's, where the star attraction was a Velasquez. Because Edward Speelman was such an eminent art dealer, I found myself sitting in the second row between the two of them. The auction room was packed, and it was possibly the first time that there were television screens in the outer rooms, with Christie's representatives on telephones taking bids worldwide. The auctioneer that day was Patrick Lindsay, brilliant at his job, and he cut a most handsome and imposing figure as he mounted the rostrum. He surveyed the scene, panning the room from underneath his large eyebrows. Everyone who was anyone in the art world was there. He looked well pleased. Suddenly his gaze settled on me, and unfortunately for him his microphone was already switched on.

'What the bloody hell do you think you're doing up at the front?'

'I may decide to bid,' I said.

'You'd better not,' he growled.

The Velasquez was sold for a world record price of two million three hundred thousand pounds. If I had been brave enough to take an enormous gamble, I need have done nothing else in life – that picture now is worth in excess of fifty million.

CHAPTER 12

A PINK TICKET OR TWO

MEANWHILE, THINGS continued to go well at our Piccadilly office. Money was flowing in, and Michael, Jake and I were not only solvent, but able to put cash away. I sold my flat in Walpole Street, and bought 63 Limerston Street in Chelsea. Annie was a brilliant interior decorator, and it was not long before our new nest was looking superb.

Soon after moving in, we decided to have some people for dinner, despite the fact that we had no dining chairs. It was all rather Bohemian, with everyone lounging around on enormous cushions. On the walls of our drawing room was a very pretty pleated fabric, and when the two of us had a final look round before our guests arrived, we were well pleased. During that afternoon one of the girls had telephoned me to say that she would be unable to come. I rang Anne at Vogue, who said that shouldn't be a problem since she was at that moment photographing a really stunning German model, Danielle, and she would ask her to come to the party. We sat her next to Mark Birley and Peter Irwin. Peter is a most straight and upright man, and with an excellent sense of humour. Danielle's English was very poor, but Peter was bowled over by this girl, who had turned up in a very small chamois leather top and matching mini skirt, with a large area of naked brown midriff. As I was taking away the plates after the first course, I saw Danielle rolling a joint. She lit up, took a large drag and offered it to Peter.

'No thanks, Danielle, not for me.'

'You no smoke then, Peter?'

'Just occasionally in Scotland, to keep the midges away.'

'You English, I no understand you at all.'

It was at our next dinner party that my old friend Nicholas Soames became a hero to us. One of the candles tipped over, and no one noticed that the material on the walls had caught fire. Nicholas was the first to spot it, and with great presence of mind he picked up a rug from the floor, and, with his arms outstretched, leaned his full weight over the flames; they pretty soon gave up the ghost. Only a couple of weeks later, he again came to Anne's rescue. We were at a dance given by Michael White at the Lyceum Ballroom. Nicholas was dancing with Anne, and, by a miracle, he happened to glance upwards at the moment one of the ceiling supporting-beams came crashing down. He hurled himself and Anne out of the way, and the beam missed them both by a whisker. Amazingly, no one was badly hurt, but I really believe that both Anne and Nicholas would have been killed if he had been less quick-witted.

That summer I went to the Eton Ramblers Annual Dinner, and (not really my fault) committed a monster faux pas. Two thirds of the way through the evening I received a note signed by the President, 'Buns' Cartwright, asking me to propose the toast of the over 1960s, and make a short address. Moments later, I banged my knife on my wine glass, and launched into a ten-minute effort, with a couple of risqué jokes. When I sat down, there was almost complete silence, and my neighbours asked me what had possessed me to make a speech. I produced the piece of paper from my pocket, and at the same time caught the eye of Edward Lane Fox, further down the table. He was in fits; it was he who had forged the note – his duplicity had worked a treat.

I had bought Limerston Street for £26,000, and we were there for four years. During this time I became a father, with the birth of Alexander on the 5th July 1973. We employed a couple of hopeless nannies during his first eighteen months, and then along came Nanny Lacey. She had excellent references, and we thought our problems were solved. But Nanny Lacey, although a conscientious woman, turned out to be completely impossible for me to live with. She was a ripping snob, and never stopped telling us how wonderful her previous employer, Lord Wimborne, had been. His name cropped up every five minutes, and he was held as a shining example against my inadequacies. The other thing that infuriated me was that Nanny would never address herself directly to me, but would always talk through Alexander. Viz: I came home at about seven o'clock one morning after a very long session of poker, only to find Nanny Lacey putting Alexander in his pram in the hallway for an unbelievably early stroll. 'Oh Alexander, here comes Daddy. Tell Daddy that we hope he's won some money at last. He has probably forgotten that he's two months in arrears with my pay.' In fact I had had a very bad night, and I was in a filthy temper. So I am afraid I looked into the pram and said, 'Alexander, why don't you tell Nanny to sod off?' Nanny Lacey screeched, 'Lord Wimborne never spoke to me like that. I will not stay here a minute longer. I have never been so insulted.' With that, she went upstairs, packed her bags and was gone.

Alexander was christened at Farm Street Church by a splendid monk called Father Ambrose. His god-parents were Rupert Lycett Green, Victoria Schott (soon to be married to Evelyn de Rothschild), Robin Hambro (wife of Rupert), Jake Morley, Serena McConnell, and Stoker Hartington.

On the nights that I had a 'pink ticket' I occasionally used to revisit some very jolly drinking clubs – Miranda's Marina in Soho was one, and the Georgian Pussy Club was another. The great advantage of the latter was that it closed at twelve o'clock. Charles Churchill used to take Anne and me to both The Palladium, and also to Danny La Rue's. Charles was a great friend of Danny's, and we were always sure of the best table and a great time. We also went to *L'Aperitif* a lot, so much so that we were invited by the management to go on the restaurant's very last evening, prior to the bulldozers moving in the following morning. That was quite a party, because we were encouraged to smash everything which had not already been removed. Within a month, the whole building was demolished.

Meanwhile, our business went from strength to strength, and we had a great team working with us. Steve Barber was only 17, but he became a really astute trader in twelve months. Charlie Macmillan was another splendid cog in the wheel. He had a ready smile, and worked all hours of the day and night. A very sparky South African girl had joined us. Penny Mackenzie was perfect: very efficient, sexy, and excellent at looking after our clients.

By this stage we were driving some fancy cars. Jake had a Ferrari, and I had a Mercedes 300SEL, while Michael Doxford had two or three, including a Bentley. I believe that many people in the City resented the three upstarts in Piccadilly, when the economy was in such appalling shape. Anne and I moved from Limerston Street, when we bought Rupert Hambro's house in Argyll Road, West Kensington. Jake moved into a large house in Tregunter Road, while Michael was living in style in Cottesmore Gardens. It was my responsibility to bring in new business, and this I did by travelling to Germany, France, and South Africa. Michael and Jake were busy in the Far East and Australia, and they had opened a successful office in Bahrain. My visits to South Africa, in particular, were great fun, and I was easily able to combine business with pleasure. I was amazed how kind and friendly everyone was, and while I was down there I played a lot of golf and made some long-lasting friends.

I used to stay in the Carlton Hotel, on the top floor of which was a very trendy nightclub. It was here that I had possibly my best ever stroke of luck. I was sitting at the bar soon after arriving in South Africa late one night, when I was approached by two girls, who asked if they could join me. They were attractive nineteen-year-old Australian twins, who were travelling slowly around the world. We had a marvelous night, one thing led to another, and the next morning I found it very hard to leave them both tucked up, in order to get to my first appointment. I could hardly wait for the evening, and I settled into the same table as I had been at the night before, full of anticipation. Alas, lightning doesn't strike twice, and I never saw the twins again.

Michael Doxford had bought himself part of an island in the Bahamas called Stocking Island, and it was there that he spent his winter holiday. He would invite two or three friends, and one or two of his best clients, to come out for a couple of weeks. One of these fellows was an Italian – I'll call him Antonio – and his business was pretty important to us. On one occasion, a large bonfire had been built just on the edge of the shore, at the bottom of Michael's garden, waiting to be lit a couple of days later, on November 5th. Antonio arrived late one night from Miami, and went for a swim before crashing out on his bed, exhausted. The next morning one of Michael's young sons, seeing the bonfire, decided to put a match to it. The fire was roaring away when Antonio came rushing out of the house and down the lawn in his underpants. He desperately tried to put the flames out by taking apart the log pile as fast as he could. It was to no avail, and he singed himself badly in his incredibly strenuous efforts. The rest of the party were having breakfast, and could not understand what all the commotion was about, although Michael was mildly upset that his son had lit the bonfire two days before Guy Fawkes night. Anyway, Antonio came disconsolately back to the house, covered in soot and with burnt eyebrows. It was only a couple of days later that he told us he had hidden two bags of cannabis under the bonfire when he went down to swim the night before. Like the timber, they had gone up in smoke.

Our office party that year took place on a boat Michael had rented off the Isle of Wight. He had placed a large dredger about a hundred yards away, and hired a professional firework man to give the most amazing display after our buffet dinner. The party went on and on and many of us drank far too much. We had recently taken on some young blood in the office, one of whom was a splendid man called Timmy Hanbury. Although he never seemed to go to bed, he would always arrive at the office on time at nine o'clock, admittedly looking as if he had just crawled out of a sack of flour – but he was never late.

At the end of this long night, Timmy and I had to make our way back to the mainland by hiring a water taxi, and then we had a short walk to our hotel. I was completely gone by this stage, and thinking I was in my bedroom, I got undressed in the lift. We reached the eighth floor, and Timmy looked round to help me out. He was amazed to see that I hadn't got a stitch on, and that I was in the process of neatly folding my trousers and shirt in the corner. To his horror at that moment the lift doors shut, leaving me on the inside and Timmy in the passage. As I began to descend, I too realised what had tran-spired. Moments later the doors opened, and there in front of me was an elderly couple who had come off an early ferry, and were on their way to their bedroom. They looked gobsmacked to see this naked figure desperately trying to close the doors manually. At that moment, they did shut and I began to ascend again. The good Timmy had been leaning on the 'up' button from the moment I had left him. I reckoned that the old couple might report me to the concièrge, so I hid in Timmy's cupboard and would not go next door. Sure enough, about ten minutes later, a small search party went into my room, and we heard the night porter say to the couple that there was no one to be found – they must have been imagin-ing things.

CHAPTER 13

THE WRONG SIDE OF THE LAW

VIRTUALLY EVERY YEAR from the mid 1960s I had been invited to shoot grouse at Bolton Abbey, in Yorkshire, and in August 1971, I was staying with my old pal Alec Montgomerie, shooting his moors in Ayrshire, when I got a surprise call on the second evening asking if I could come down to Yorkshire that night. My father and Alec's father, with three or four of their friends, had just started dinner when I took the call, and I was expected to shoot the next day with them. But, when Stoker Hartington rang me I knew by the excitement in his voice, that the following day at Bolton Abbey could be exceptional, so I broke all the rules and said I would get in my car and drive down that night. I walked back into the dining room and told my dad and my host that I wouldn't be there the next day, as I was going to go to Yorkshire. My father exploded, and said something to the effect that he had always taught me the unbreakable rule that you did not accept something, only to cancel when you got a better invitation. I reckoned the day in Ayrshire would probably end up with about thirty brace of grouse, so, knowing that I would incur my dad's wrath, I got in my car and drove south. The next day we had a post-war record at Bolton Abbey, killing a thousand and thirteen grouse. That evening I rang my father, who would not take the call. He merely handed the telephone to Alec's dad, George Kidston-Montgomerie. I asked him how they had got on and he said they had had a very nice day, and what a pity I hadn't been there. They had shot twenty-two and a half brace. He then said to me 'Was your trip worth it?'

'Well,' I said, 'we killed five hundred and six and a half brace.'

There was an exclamation at the other end, then a pause and the admirable colonel said, 'Well done, boy. You did absolutely the right thing.'

It was Stoker who took me one evening to a Fishmongers' Dinner in the summer of 1974. His father was Prime Warden, and he thought it would be fun for me to go and see a big Livery Dinner. There were seven glasses in front of me when I sat down. As the evening wore on, more and more fine wines were poured into one glass after another, and I felt my head beginning to swim. About six months before that, the drink-driving law had been passed for the first time, but foolishly, I still drove back to Limerston Street, with Stoker in the passenger seat. Soon after we left the Fishmongers' Hall I realised there was a police car on my tail. If I say it myself, I drove slowly and well, and arrived home without incident. I had gone up the steps to my house, when the police car drew up and I was asked whether I was the driver of the vehicle. 'No,' I said, 'This fellow was driving,' pointing at poor Stoker and throwing him the keys. The copper didn't believe me, but to be on the safe side he put us both in the back of his wagon and took us off to Savile Row police station. There I cooled my heels in a cell for several hours, sticking out like a sore thumb in my white tie and tails, while the gallant Stoker waited in an outer room to see what would be the outcome. My fellow inmates (all prostitutes) asked me where I had been, all dressed up like that.

'I've been to a Fishmongers' Dinner,' I slurred.

'Ooh,' they giggled, ''e don't look like a fishmonger to us.'

I had a blood test, and at about four o'clock in the morning was told that I could go home (providing I didn't drive) since the result would not be ready for three days. I had to report to the court the following day to hear my charge.

I went with a policeman to find my friend and the two of us got in a cab and went home. The next day I was told by the beak to come back three days later to the same court, at which point my blood test result would be known. I had dressed myself up to look pretty smart, and while waiting, I was seated next to a real old-fashioned drunk. When I returned on the third day, this character was there again, and I found myself next to him once more. I felt sorry for him, and thought how sad his life must be; at which point he shoved his index finger at me and said to his pal, 'Bloody 'ell, you see the same poofs every time you come 'ere.' I lost my licence for a year, and it was a salutary lesson.

My Monday evenings were spent playing poker at the Turf Club, in Carlton House Terrace. There were at least a dozen keen members so getting together the required number of five or six players was not a problem. We used to start at eight in the evening and have a late sandwich dinner with plenty of good wine. The biggest winner at the end of the session paid the entire bar bill. The Turf Club was full of like-minded people and was always an enjoyable place to be. There was a wonderful barman, Jimmie Holland, and a famous Hall Porter, Mr Grace. One of his jobs was to telephone Alexander Hesketh, a young Member who was studying in America, every afternoon at 2pm. The ringing tone was Alexander's early-morning alarm call and as he never picked up the receiver, he did not incur a bill. Years later, when Alexander built a new Members' Stand at his Towcester Racecourse he named it after his friend and ally. It is still called The Grace Stand.

So, in 1974, everything in my life was going right. I had a wonderful, loving and beautiful wife; I had a one-year-old son; I had a brilliant job, working with great friends and making good money; and outside working hours I was having as good a time as one could imagine. But as so often happens when everything looks set fair, my world would shortly change dramatically – the switchback was about to make a sharp descent.

CHAPTER 14

A DEAD SHARK AND A
FOX'S BRUSH

IN JULY 1974 Anne and I went on holiday to the Lido in Venice. We stayed at an hotel with a large swimming pool, and were much looking forward to our week away. Alexander had been left in the capable hands of a nanny and I had asked her to telephone me each morning about mid-day, just to make sure that everything was in order at home.

We were soaking up the sun, me looking very white compared with all the Italians, and the other guests who had been at the hotel for a week or two, when a loudspeaker crackled 'Il Signor Pèto e desiderato urgentemente al telefono.' Knowing it would be our nanny I hopped off my chair, and walked briskly round to the bar to take the call. I was well aware that everyone else was now sitting up, looking at me as I progressed. The following morning at exactly mid-day the same announcement was made over the loudspeaker. Once again, I jumped off my chair and walked right round the swimming pool to the bar. This time everyone (possibly three hundred people) began to laugh, and I felt extremely self-conscious. On the third day the same announcement came over the tannoy, and as I made my way to the telephone, there was even more amusement. I said to the barman, who spoke good English, 'Why does everyone think I'm such a joke? I know that I am pale and partly burnt, and don't have a hell of a figure, but surely it can't be this that they are laughing at?'

'Well,' said the barman, 'we just want to see if you are living up to your name.'

'What on earth do you mean?' I said.

'Don't you know that, in Italian, Peto means fart?'

After that episode, I have tried to avoid holidays in Italy.

That autumn I decided to take up hunting again, and bought a nice six-year-old called *Henry* whom I had arranged to stable at Dean Manor, near Chipping Norton, with Lucinda Marchessini. I had first met Lucinda thirteen years before, when she came to stay with her brother-in-law, Harry Erne, at Crom Castle in County Fermanagh, and I was stationed at Castle Archdale. She was an incredibly good looking girl, with an irresistible figure, and had told me at that time that she had just got engaged to a Greek called Demetri. I met her again years later at a party in London, and was immediately smitten. Lucinda was a marvellous athlete, a low handicap golfer, and a near-Olympic standard dressage rider. By this stage, she was divorced from Demetri, after giving him four girls – Lucinda, Cassandra, Atalanta, and Tatiana who were now aged between five and ten years old.

I would go down to Dean once a week, and stay the night before hunting with the Heythrop. The inevitable happened, and Lucinda and I began an affair, at the very outset of which, she said that on no account was I ever to think of marrying her, because although she was a first-rate mistress, she would not be a good wife. Certainly she had a solipsistic view of life, and at that time she was completely immersed in her horses, and her children.

On one of my trips to South Africa, I arranged for her to come out and join me at the seaside resort of Plettenberg Bay which in those days was a lovely unknown village, with only one hotel, the Beacon Island, one little French restaurant and a beautiful beach. I reckoned there would be no chance of our being discovered there. After checking in, we got into the lift, and who should come in behind us but the man who had been my Chairman at G W Joynson, Jock Mocatta. 'Hello Nick,' he said, 'how's your wife?' I jerked my head in Lucinda's direction, and he rather belatedly twigged and gave me a knowing wink. When I went back to London, I discovered that he had died on his way home, so miraculously our secret was still safe.

The management had placed signs everywhere that guests must be especially careful where they swam, since the prevailing wind had brought many sharks close to the shore, (though there was, of course, a comprehensive shark net right around the area designated for swimming.) Lucinda was never very bold in the sea, and on our first afternoon she tiptoed gingerly into the water. When she was about waist deep she rushed splashing back to me, and squawked hysterically that she had just seen a shark. 'Nonsense,' I said, 'you're imagining things.' I waded boldly in and had not taken many paces when I too saw it. I was transfixed, for its head was only a yard or so away from my feet. At that moment it rolled over in the water, and I immediately realised it must be dead – it had probably been nudged under the nets by the current. I grabbed it by the narrow bit just in front of its tail, and yelled 'Shark, shark, shark!'

The two hundred or so swimmers looked towards me, and saw that I was wrestling half submerged with this beast. To a man, they fled out of the sea way up onto the beach. I had a tremendous battle with this great fish, its fin sometimes above the water and sometimes beneath. But after about three minutes I delivered a couple of *coups de grâce*, with the side of my right hand behind its head and threw it back into the ocean, and walked out of the sea, slapping my hands together to rid them of the sand and slime. The movie *Jaws* had recently hit all the cinemas worldwide, so sharks were very much on everyone's mind. I was immediately surrounded by a throng of bathers, who all cheered me, and were very excited by my amazing bravery. We went back to the hotel, and later Lucinda and I were fêted with free drinks, before dinner. While we dined, she said to me 'I've been thinking about that shark. Was it by chance already dead when you started your fight with it?'

'Of course it was,' I said, 'but for goodness sake don't tell anyone else, or the free cocktails will dry up very quickly.'

Our week together was idyllic, as we basked in the sunshine and also in our fellow guests' admiration.

Sunny Marlborough had recently married a delightful Swedish girl called Rosita and one evening after a good day's hunting she was presented with the fox's brush. About a week later I had the most extraordinary telephone conversation with her. She rang me up and in broken English said 'Hello Neek, I am very worried about my bush. I have tried pickling it in aspic in order to preserve it, but it is now very smelly.' I really had no idea what she was talking about – Sunny has picked a rum one this time, I thought – but as she rambled on I suddenly realised that she thought she had been given the fox's bush, rather than its brush. 'Don't worry about your bush,' I said, 'just hang it outside somewhere for a few days and it will dry out, and then it will stop smelling.'

Not long after this Rosita's sister and her husband, Prince Max of Bavaria, were staying at Blenheim for a shooting party. They brought two beautiful daughters with them, and another German couple. Nicholas Soames and I were there, and were surprised at dinner when all the visitors started chatting away in German. Nicholas kept quiet for about ten minutes, and then suddenly banged the table with his fist. 'Bloody hell,' he bellowed, 'we won the first round, AND the replay. I certainly didn't expect to hear German spoken at Winston Churchill's birthplace. Please revert to English.' Dead silence, except for Sunny's and my suppressed laughter.

I had a very unfortunate accident that autumn. I was staying at Ginge with William and Annabel Astor, for a shooting weekend. The previous week, he had taken delivery of one of the very first Range Rovers, and it was his pride and joy, but sadly, he had a broken leg and so was unable to drive it. He asked me to do the honours, and I had the beautiful Ward sisters, Rachel and Tracy, as my passengers. It was an incredibly cold day, and we were all thankful when we came in for lunch. Unknown to me, while we were inside there was a heavy sleet storm, and the particles froze as soon as they hit the ground. We set off after lunch across a very large grass field. I don't know why, but I thought it might be amusing to drive towards the one and only telegraph pole in the middle of the field, and then jink this great car, at the last minute. Of course, I did not realise I was driving on sheet ice. There was no jink; I ran straight into the pole. The girls and the guns fell all over the place, and the bonnet of the vehicle flew into the air and landed behind us. William was understandably furious, and said there was no way he was going to claim under his insurance. He would get a valuation that afternoon and I would have to pay whatever the amount was before I left the next day. The figure arrived at by the garage was £1240, a hell of a lot of money. In desperation, after dinner I suggested that we had a game of poker. Many hours later I had made £1280, a good result. The bill was paid, and I had forty pounds left to tip the butler.

I organised another illicit holiday for Lucinda and myself, this time to Kenya. I made plans to stop there on my way back from South Africa; I would meet up with her and we would go on a safari together. A friend of mine, Gillies Turle, owned an antique shop in Nairobi, and he fixed up a hair-raising trip for me with a white hunter called Christopher Matchett. The plan was to go down the Tana River on an inflatable raft, with no outboard motor. The Tana flows between Somalia and Kenya; at some places it is very narrow and fast, at others it is a quarter of a mile wide and slow flowing. Lucinda was to follow in a Land Rover, along the river bank, with the three Kenyans who were looking after us. Christopher and I set off at dawn on the first morning, armed only with binoculars and a couple of paddles. The idea was to make absolutely no noise so that we could see all the birds and animals attracted by the river. There had been a drought in that part of Africa for the previous three years, which made the Tana an essential port of call for wildlife.

The next forty-eight hours were possibly the most frightening I have ever spent. We hurtled through rapids, and then we would become becalmed in a wide part of the river, only to find that we had the company of masses of partially submerged hippos. One of these enormous creatures broke the surface about five yards from our raft and opened its mouth as wide as it could. For two pins it could have waddled over and swallowed us up. We saw some large crocodiles, but they were not such a worry, since they tended to swim away when they caught sight of us. The other thing I was most alarmed about were the water snakes which swirled around our raft. The possibility of capsizing didn't bear thinking about.

On that first evening, we met up with Lucinda and the boys, and pitched a very rudimentary camp. Just before we went to bed, Christopher said he thought he had seen a crocodile about thirty yards below our tents, and that it would not be safe to go to sleep. He gave me a rifle, with night sights, and said if I saw it I was to shoot it. He sat a little away from me, also with a rifle. There was a moon, but for a while I could see absolutely nothing, despite peering endlessly in the direction of the suspect. I raised my rifle to make sure I could see through the sights, and to my amazement, only about twenty yards away from me, I could unmistakably see the croc's two eyes. I steadied myself and squeezed the trigger. There was a fantastic commotion and much splashing of water. Had I killed it? Christopher said on no account was I to move, he would have a look. He walked (I thought very foolishly) towards where all the noise had emanated, but there was no sign of a body. We went to bed, but none of us was able to get much sleep for fear that the croc might be wounded and pay us another visit. At first light, I peeped out of the flap of our tent. Nothing. So I got up and walked to the edge of the river. There was the enormous animal, mostly submerged, but stone dead.

We continued on our journey all that day and although we saw amazing sights, this was not a trip I would ever like to make again. For half an hour each morning sand grouse would come to the river, possibly as many as ten thousand of them in little family coveys. They have to touch the water with their wing tips, and are then somehow able to fly back to their feeding grounds, and to their young, with a little pool of water still intact in each wing. On the second morning, on a dead tree overhanging the river, we placed some fish we had caught on a long-line the evening before. A fish eagle which had been spiralling high above us in a thermal, saw them and went into the most incredible dive, removing one of them perfectly with its talons. Lucinda was sitting in a cotton skirt on a large rock watching this unforgettable sight. When she glanced down towards her feet she was appalled to see two scorpions advancing slowly up the rock towards her knickers.

On the third day, we reached Adamsons Falls, and by arrangement, we went to stay for twenty-four hours with the great George Adamson. There he showed us his lions; he had the most extraordinary rapport with them. Lucinda was amazed that the lavatory we had to use was an outside affair, consisting of an elephant's skull (the seat) perched over a deep pit. On the fourth morning, we set off on the five-hour drive across very rutted terrain to the nearest airstrip, and flew in a light aircraft back to Nairobi. I think we were both extremely pleased to return to civilisation. The following year Christopher Matchett was killed by some Somali tribesmen, while he was conducting a similar safari to ours. They had quietly traversed the river, and slit his throat while he was asleep. His Kenyan guards put up no resistance, and the Somalis made off with everything in his camp.

Back in England, the wheels were beginning to come off our business, and Annie was becoming more and more unhappy with me – with good reason. At Doxfords, we had expanded into two or three other businesses, and these were swallowing a great deal of money. Michael Doxford was an entrepreneur with a great flair, and in fact each of these ventures became successful, but long after we had had to say goodbye to them. By this stage Michael had moved the office to 10 St James's Street, on which we had bought a long lease for just under a million pounds; had we been able to hang onto it, it would have been yet another excellent long-term investment.

We had rented a pheasant shoot at Cocking in Sussex; the plan was to entertain our clients, as well as enjoying it ourselves. The first time I went there, I got lost and was very late. Finally I saw some landrovers parked by the side of the road. In the distance I could see the guns climbing up towards their pegs for the first drive. There was a man standing by the vehicles, and I told him I was one of the shooters. He said it was probably too late to catch everyone up for this drive, as they had all drawn their numbers and suggested I went about fifty yards towards them and stood by a gate, in order to intercept any birds they missed. I was behind number eight gun, with all the rest above me and out to my left. There was a strong wind blowing to the right, so I reckoned that the man in front of me would get quite a bit of shooting. I leaned against the gate post and settled down to wait. Very soon birds poured out of the wood up on the skyline. Initially, they made for the middle of the line, but soon they were caught in the wind and headed towards my man. It transpired that he was a complete non-striker, and I had a marvellous shoot. At the end of the drive I picked up my birds, put them in a pile, and went back to my car. It was only when the other guns began arriving that I realised I had never seen any of them in my life. I was with the wrong shoot. The host was not pleased, and asked me how many birds I had shot. I told him nineteen, at which he was even more upset, because apparently they had bought a day where only one hundred and fifty were to be shot in total. I beat a hasty retreat, and finally found Michael, Jake and my friends.

At the end of November 1976 Lucinda and I embarked on a Sponges Sporting Tour with four of our hunters. We set off for Leicestershire, where our first day was to be with the Quorn. Travelling in the horse box were Fiona McMeekan, who was looking after the horses, and Tim Hudson, in charge of our clothes, boots etc. Lucinda and I went on ahead by car. Our second day was with the Belvoir Hunt, and we woke to a very misty morning. The Meet was at Wartnaby, the home of John King who was then Hunt Chairman. Because it was so foggy, we had to hang around waiting for the weather to improve, and we had some drinks in his drawing room. Prince

Charles was there, and I suspect the day would have been cancelled if he had not been. I found myself talking to an old fellow called Lord Daresbury and mentioned that Lucinda's grandfather had been a Master of the Belvoir.

'I doubt that,' he said, 'what was his name?'

I said 'He was called Marshall Roberts, sir'.

'Ah yes,' he said, 'Marshall Roberts, 1922 to 1924. No offence meant, but if he'd been a dog hound I wouldn't have bred from it.'

We did eventually move off, and had a tremendous hunt in the late afternoon. There was a very pretty girl out, and she went brilliantly across country. I was on a marvellous new horse of mine called *Marble Arch*. He was 17.2hh, half Cleveland Bay and half thoroughbred. He had enormous presence and was the best hunter I ever owned. This girl rode up beside me late that evening, and she said, 'I have been watching you, and I can't make up my mind which of you likes to show off most, you or your horse.' Sadly, at that point she went home, and I never even learnt her name.

That evening, the four of us, with the four horses, set off for a day in Yorkshire, and then ended up having two days in Northumberland with the Percy – thereby hunting five days out of six. I shall never forget the feudal sight of the Duke of Northumberland's chauffeur, stopping the traffic in both directions on the A1 as hounds, huntsmen and followers jogged unimpeded across the main road. We all returned to Dean exhausted, but in one piece.

By mid-1977 Doxfords was really beginning to struggle, and the three of us were having to cut back on our expenditure. However, I had bought, in partnership with Lucinda, a two-year-old colt by *Homeric* out of *Bold Over*, which we called *Home Run*. We sent him to be trained by Jeremy Tree at Beckhampton. *Home Run* turned out to be an extremely good animal. He won his two prep races, and then the Philips Electrical Stakes over seven furlongs at Ascot by seven lengths from *Julio Mariner* and *Dactylogropher* – both of whom later won Classic races.

Home Run was then headed for a Group One race at Doncaster in October, in those days called the *William Hill Futurity*, and worth £40,000 to the winner. Unfortunately, the heavens opened for twenty-four hours before the race, and the going was bottomless. Lester Piggott was on board, and gave our colt an extremely hard race, just beaten into third place by a head, and a short head. After the Ascot race, *Home Run* had been 14–1 ante-post favourite for the 1978 Derby. We were offered a lot of money for him then, but foolishly, and arrogantly, turned it down. *Home Run* ran only twice as a three-year-old, finishing a close third in the *Tote Free Handicap* at Newmarket, and again finishing third in the *Predominate* at Goodwood. After this race he was found to have broken down, and was ultimately sold to India as a stallion, where he had much success.

Because of my ever-increasing involvement with Lucinda, Anne quite rightly told me that our marriage had run its course. It was a dreadfully distressing time, made more so because Anne is such a gentle, loyal person. In February 1979, Lucinda and I were married, and I moved into Dean Manor.

In the August of the previous summer, I had been back again to Bolton Abbey. Jake Morley was also there, and Stoker's younger sister Sophy had asked three young men. These fellows were incredibly polite, and they shot well. Jake came up to me on the second evening and said that we were going to have to mind our Ps and Qs, or we might find ourselves not invited in years to come, being superseded by these twenty-five-year-olds. I said that I would try to put a stop to that, and luckily my chance came the very next morning. One of the young men, Nigel Galliers-Pratt, came up to me before breakfast and mentioned that he had lost his cap. It was pouring with rain outside, and I told him to take the one hanging on the antlers. I said that it was specially put there for guests who had come without any headgear. He was enormously grateful, and put on Andrew Devonshire's cap. A few minutes later Nigel asked me if I knew in which car he would be travelling up to the moor. I told him that shortly a Bentley would appear, and I suggested that he got into the front passenger seat next to Joe, the chauffeur. I said that the Duke always sat in the back (which he never did), and particularly liked a spirited conversation all the way up to the grouse shoot (which he hated). 'Well, that's really kind of you,' said Nigel. As soon as the black Bentley appeared I ushered Nigel into the front seat. Moments later there was a bellow in the hall and the Duke was asking Henry, the butler, if he had seen his cap.

'No, Your Grace. I'm sure it was hanging in its usual place earlier this morning.'

'I believe I saw Nigel Galliers-Pratt wearing a cap very similar to yours,' I murmured.

'Well, where is the fellow?'

'The most extraordinary thing is that he is sitting in the front of your Bentley, Andrew,' I said.

'Well, get him out of there. What on earth's he doing in my seat?'

So I went to the car, and pulled Nigel out. 'What do you think you are doing?' I said. 'That's the Duke's seat – get out immediately.'

Poor Nigel looked thoroughly bemused, and not a little shaken.

About twelve years after this incident I was walking down the beach in Barbados towards the Sandy Lane Hotel, hoping for a pre-lunch drink. There was a barrier across the sand with a large black security man standing by it. 'You can't come in heah, suh, unless you are a resident, or unless you know some-one stayin' heah.' I spied Nigel lying on a sun lounger next to his wife. 'I know that man very well,' I said, 'he'll vouch for me, I'm sure.' So the security man went over to Nigel. After a brief conversation, Nigel came up to the barrier, smoking his habitual cigar, looked me straight in the eye and said over his shoulder to the security guard 'I've never seen this man before in my life.' He then laughed, and said, 'I've been waiting to get my own back on you for a good many years, and now I feel we are quits!'

Jake Morley and I were in an August houseparty at Invermark Lodge, in Angus. Sarah Keswick was our hostess and she begged us to behave ourselves. It transpired that the Queen and Prince Philip were coming to shoot with Sarah's parents, the Dalhousies, the following week. All went well until the last evening when we were to attend the ghillie's dance, a ceilidh. As a rather bad joke I popped one of the fire extin-guishers into Jake's bed before we set off, and thought no more about it. Needless to say, when we returned in the early hours the beastly thing had gone off. The mattress and carpet had become saturated with foam, and the floor was beginning to buckle. Sarah was apoplectic. After much squeezing and brushing and washing the room began to look more reasonable – but it was a night with no sleep, and many raised voices.

Jake had taken a shine to one of the girls at the ceilidh, and had danced with her for the greater part of the evening. He told her that if she ever found herself in London to be sure to look him up. Only a week later, he returned to Tregunter Road after work at about 7pm. His wife, Kirsty, opened the door, and said frostily, 'There's a girl from Scotland to see you in the drawing room.' This was a tricky situation, not made easier by Kirsty insisting that Jake take the poor lass out to dinner, since she had travelled so far to see him. 'You forgot to mention that you were married,' murmured the girl in her very Scottish brogue. The meal was not a resounding success.

CHAPTER 15

'TIME, LIKE AN EVER-ROLLING STREAM, BEARS ALL ITS SONS AWAY.'

M L DOXFORD & CO. finally ceased trading at the end of 1979. There was a blaze of publicity when the company went into receivership, including features on two editions of *The Money Programme*, and much comment in the press. In fact, when all our assets, such as the leasehold on 10 St. James's Street, were sold and when our personal guarantees were called in, our indebtedness was just over one million pounds. Nowadays, I don't imagine that would even merit a footnote in the *Financial Times*, but because we had enjoyed flamboyant lifestyles the press really went to town, and gave us a most unpleasant ride. We had at least been on the pitch for a time, while most of our detractors had merely been on the touchline.

As far as I personally was concerned, the unlimited guarantee I had signed in the early 70's cost me virtually everything I possessed. I had already sold my house in Argyll Road, Kensington, the previous year, in order to provide Annie with some money when we were divorced. I was lucky, in that, when Doxford's went down, I was already living in Dean Manor, on the edge of the Cotswolds. However, I had no income, no job, and no way of paying the substantial bills which running a country house entails. I went to see Lucinda's ex-husband, Demetri. He could not have been more accommodating. He told me to send all bills relevant to the house and garden to him and made it easy for me, by saying that he thought it was the right thing to do, bearing in mind that Dean was the home of his four daughters. For the next few years, I felt in some ways more married to Demetri than to Lucinda, but the arrangement worked well, and there was never a hiccup over finance. Without him I would have been a mendicant.

Demetri kept his magnificent collection of wine in the cellar at Dean, and on one occasion I did use one of his bottles to entertain an old friend of mine. It never occurred to me that he would check up, since he seldom came down to the country. How wrong I was; unknown to me Demetri kept a meticulous cellar book. On his next visit to see his girls, he quietly asked me to replace the missing bottle of Haut Brion '61. Surprisingly, our close friendship survived.

With so much time on my hands, I found myself hunting at least twice a week on my two lovely horses, *Marble Arch* and *Willie*. Lucinda spent several hours each day training her dressage horses, and being given tuition on them by her trainer, Ferdi Eilberg.

After a lapse of nine years, I returned to the River Naver in the summer of 1979. I took with me my seventy-six-year-old mother, and my six-year-old son Alexander. Jake Morley also joined us. We had a very happy week; my mama caught a twenty-pound salmon on her little trout rod, and it took her four hours to land it. Until the last day there was not much water in the river, but the day before we left there was a storm and everything looked perfect for our final afternoon, when the river began to settle again. The rule on the Naver was that only one man and one woman could fish at the same time. Jake and I had each caught a salmon that afternoon, and as darkness fell we could see a run of fish entering the pool where we were, on number two beat. I said to Jakie that we had both better have a go, and hope that no one was looking. I borrowed my mother's headscarf and waded into the middle of the river, fairly sure that from a distance and in the gloaming I would look like a woman. As ill luck would have it Jake and I both hooked salmon exactly when the river superintendent, a very punchy Wing Commander, was driving home down the Strath. He stopped his car, got out his night binoculars, and immediately smelt a rat. However, the road was on the opposite side of the river to us and about half a mile away, so that he did not come and accost us immediately. Nevertheless, just prior to our departure on t he Sunday morning the Wing Co. appeared at the front door of Skelpick Lodge. 'I believe that you and your male friend were both fishing the river at the same time last evening,' he said. I looked him straight in the eye, and lied. 'Well,' he said, 'I understand you were in the Forces like me, and therefore, as an officer and a gentleman, I know you cannot be lying to me. However, if you should ever come up here again, I would ask you to be more circumspect.' I felt very small indeed, and have often thought of that embarrassing conversation.

Being up on the Naver again brought back so many wonderful memories of my youth, when I had visited several years running with Henry Lopes. But the Naver and its owners had changed during the ensuing time. There were new, affluent proprietors, who knew little of the river and its ways, and even less of the people who worked there. The sole aim seemed to be to catch as much as possible, and to fish from dawn to dusk, day in and day out. Like so many sporting activities, the river had become commercialised, and its charm had inevitably suffered as a result.

In March 1980 my father died, aged eighty three. He had been a strong influence in my life, and his straightforwardness and sense of humour were a great example to us. I visited him in Basingstoke Hospital a couple of days before the end. When I went into his room, he appeared to be asleep but had a smile on his craggy face. When he opened his eyes, I said 'What were you thinking of just now? It seemed to be making you very happy; I wonder if you can remember?' My father said 'I was trying to re-live some of the most amusing episodes in my life. Shall I tell you the one I had in my mind just now?' 'Please do,' I said. My father told me the following story. At the end of 1917 he had been with the Ninth Lancers in France. He had some leave due to him, and was given the address of a house of ill repute in Paris, where it was suggested that he might have his first experience with a member of the opposite sex. My father told me that he was just about to do the deed, when he heard the unmistakable voice of his Commanding Officer, Colonel Cavendish, in the next cubicle. The Colonel growled 'Mademoiselle, mademoiselle, ouvrez les jambes, vous avez cassez mon pince-nez.' My dad was so appalled at the thought of what was going on a few feet away from him that he left the bordello still a virgin.

My mother and father had been married for forty-six years, and she was distraught at his passing.

My father once told me that he had never really seen eye to eye with his elder brother, Michael, but he had been persuaded by my mama to spend a weekend with him and Frances, his sister-in-law. They arrived at Iford Manor, near Bradford-on-Avon, at about six o'clock on the Friday evening. After a while my father and mother went upstairs, and he began to run a bath before dinner. The plumbing in the house was ancient, and as my father bent down to put in the large plug, gurgling up the waste pipe came his brother's voice. 'You take over before dinner Frances, because I've had enough of them already.'

My dad was quintessentially a soldier and a countryman. Without fail he was charming and helpful to all the friends I brought back to his house, and despite many provocations he always forgave and saw the funny side. I missed him enormously.

CHAPTER 16

BUTTERFLIES IN
THE SUN

THE FALL-OUT OF the Doxford and Co. collapse continued and for nearly two years I was without a job. But, early in
1981, my old school friend Simon Keswick wrote to me from
his office in Hong Kong, offering me a position with one of
his subsidiaries, Jardine Glanvill & Co, the insurance broker.
This was a splendid gesture, and a lifeline which I grabbed
with both hands. I began to commute to their small office in
Gloucester to learn the business, and about a year later, joined
their City branch.

Life at Dean was idyllic. Lucinda and I threw ourselves
into the creation of a splendid garden. The main herbaceous
border was nearly four metres wide and about seventy metres
long, and by the end of June each year it was a magnificent
sight. We planted masses of shrub roses in other parts of the
garden, and every spare moment was spent trying to improve
the general outlook. We played tennis with the girls and then
lay by the pool – warm and careless, like butterflies in the sun.

Behind the large Cotswold wall towards the back drive, we
dug a pond, and there played host to various different types of
ducks and geese. We also loved our rare breed chickens –
Apenzellas, Houdans and Aracunas – the last named lay blue
eggs, which tends to surprise people at breakfast. Over the

next year or two we expanded our menagerie by buying two Welsh Black sheep – Mabel and Melissa. Lucinda drove to Norfolk in her old Range Rover to pick up a Welsh Black ram, in order to start our breeding flock. On her return journey, the dog guard slipped forward, and in a flash the ram was sitting next to her in the front passenger seat. As she slowed down through the towns and villages on the way home Lucinda turned even more heads than usual. We also bought a beautiful Oxford 'black and sandy' sow. We called her Priscilla, and she always followed me at heel when I was shooting pigeons in her field. If I stopped, she would sit down beside me. If I shot a bird she would trot off and pick it up. Sadly, she did not retrieve it, but invariably started eating the pigeon where it had fallen. After a few months we had a mating with a boar belonging to our neighbour, John Blackwell, and soon there were thirteen little piglets flying round their enclosure. On the other side of the road to Dean Manor there lived a charming retired Oxford Don. He spent every waking minute tending his vegetable patch, and it looked immaculate. Unfortunately, the inevitable happened. Our piglets escaped at dawn one June morning, and, when this poor fellow awoke, it was to see that his entire garden had been rootled. He begged us to come and collect the thirteen miscreants, which proved far easier said than done.

I was giving the dogs a walk last thing one evening, when I heard something grubbing around in the grassy bank to my left. It can't be those naughty piglets, I thought. I motioned quietly to the dogs to sit, and I stood still to await developments. The moon was up, and I could just make out the bottom of a large badger. He was digging for all he was worth, oblivious that he had company. Soon there was a loud buzzing noise, and I realised he was after the honey in a bee's nest. I watched quietly, and the next thing I saw was Mrs B trotting down the track towards me, with two minute children behind her. I left them having a feast, impervious to the bees all around their heads.

In the summer of 1982, I entered a Triathlon Competition, in a team with James Teacher and Amanda Hartington. The three disciplines were 1. Riding. Against the clock over a set course of obstacles. 2. Fishing. This was an accuracy test where one had to score as many 'hits' as possible by placing one's fly in a series of hoops out on the lake, and 3. Shooting. Clay pigeons were the target, and the aggregate kills by the team in two minutes was credited to the total score. We won our preliminary round at the East of England Show at Peterborough, and were extremely elated when we also won at The Royal Windsor Horse Show.

Lucinda was very into her dressage, and had a magnificent stallion called *Kasimir*, who in the end took her right up the ladder to Grand Prix. I was hunting away on a regular basis with two horses each time, and I became immersed in the Heythrop Hunt, its people, and its politics. We had four dogs, and a splendid Moroccan housekeeper called Mamas. All in all, life was grand. My four step-daughters were at Wycombe Abbey School; they were all intelligent, and by this stage were growing into the beautiful girls that they later became.

When I had been at Dean for two or three years, we decided to have a house party for Cheltenham Races in March. Two of the people we asked were Stoker and Amanda Hartington, who were to arrive after racing on the Tuesday. Unfortunately, they stayed on for drinks in someone's box until late that evening, and then got hopelessly lost trying to find their way to us. At about nine o'clock we decided to start dinner without them; when they eventually appeared, Stoker told me that he thought he had arrived, when he saw in his headlights a large house nearby in Chadlington, and had disembarked. The next day I happened to meet the owner of that house, the Duke of Leinster, walking his dogs. He told me that one of my guests had arrived and rung his doorbell, having carried the suitcases into the porch. He said, 'I was having an early night, so I came down the stairs in my dressing gown to open up. I said to your friend, 'Good Evening, I am the Duke of Leinster.' The reply he got was 'Good Evening to you Sir, I'm nearly the Duke of Devonshire, but I think I must be in the wrong house.'

In July 1983 I organised a large party, in aid of a sporting charity. I called it a Midsummer Madness, and the idea was for each group of friends to bring a picnic to the farm near Burford where the extravaganza was to be held. I had arranged a fun fair, and a small marquee with Humphrey Lyttleton and his jazz band. Otherwise the whole affair was open air. We ran three Midnight Steeplechases in fancy dress over some small obstacles. The contestants had to leap out of a double bed, put on their fancy dress, jump on their horses and complete the circuit bareback. The first person back between the sheets won the race. These competitions were floodlit, and created much excitement. The picnics that people produced were judged by the Duchess of Devonshire and Rocco Forte. The winners of the best, and most elaborate feast won the prize of two nights for four in one of Rocco's hotels in Paris. Two thousand five hundred people came to this party, and a large cheque was donated to the charity.

I continued my visits to Bolton Abbey, and in 1982 I shot there every month from August to January. The generosity and kindness of my host and hostess knew no bounds. One morning when we were in the grouse butts, it transpired that David Harlech had been shooting at grouse very close to his neighbours. One of these mentioned to Stoker that he had been petrified, and had spent most of the drive sitting in the bottom of his butt with his loader. Stoker told his father, but the situation was made all the more embarrassing, because David Harlech, who was a cousin of Andrew's, had been shooting at Bolton Abbey for about thirty years and in his day had been an exceptionally fine shot. In order to sort out the situation Andrew called the rest of the young guns to him, and said that he would talk to everybody after lunch, but we were not to worry since the razz was not directed at us. Sure enough, we were all told to gather outside the shooting hut. Andrew said 'It has been brought to my attention that one of you is firing at birds much too close to your neighbour's butt. Please be far more circumspect and err on the side of safety at all times.' At which point there was a loud ejaculation from David Harlech, who said 'Quite right Andrew, I agree with you. I think some of these young men are thoroughly dangerous.'

It was during that house party that I was told a story about another Yorkshire landlord, Sir Richard Sykes, who lived at Sledmere. He had been persuaded by his charming and worthy wife to do something they virtually never did – go out to dinner with people in an adjacent village. Sir Richard owned an enormous Cadillac, and it was with great difficulty that he negotiated his hostesses' front gateway. The lady was in a high state of nervous excitement at the imminent arrival of her smart guests. On entering the house, the Sykeses were told that dinner would be delayed for a while, as the aga was being difficult. 'Oh,' said Sir Richard, 'I thought he was still in France.' When this story was repeated later that week to Lord Derby, he said, 'I don't understand the joke. Was he in France, or wasn't he?'

Shooting any type of bird of prey had by now been made illegal; the damage inflicted on grouse stocks by hen-harriers, peregrines and sparrow hawks is enormous. An American said to me that he thought we were all too law-abiding. 'In Montana the rule is shoot 'n shovel,' he said. 'Well, don't even *think* about it over here,' I replied.

Stoker always liked to ensure that his shooting parties went well, and was sad if a guest went to bed too early. One evening, a year or two later, I had a splitting headache and as everyone headed for the billiard room to play billiard fives, I thought I would sneak off to bed – despite the fact it was only eleven o'clock. I was fairly sure that Stoker would come to find me later on when he realised I was missing. Each bedroom door has a little slot in which is placed a card with the name of the guest, and on an impulse I decided to change my name card with that of my neighbour. I had never met Angus Ogilvy before that evening, but he was the unlucky recipient of my ruse. I went to bed and had eight hours uninterrupted sleep. I was sitting at breakfast the next morning reading the newspaper, when down the spiral stone staircase came Sir Angus, very slowly, and still in his dressing gown. 'My goodness, Angus, what on earth has happened to you?' said our hostess. 'Well,' he replied, 'it was one of the strangest things. At two o'clock this morning, while I was in a deep sleep, my door was flung open, someone shouted "You little wimp," and took a flying leap from the doorway on to the top of my bed. Unfortunately he landed in the small of my back, and I am afraid as a result I don't think I'll be able to come out shooting this morning.' 'Good heavens,' said Debo, 'I am so awfully sorry.' At that moment Stoker came past my chair, bent down and whispered in my ear, 'I'll see you later.'

Another surprising episode on the moor came a couple of weeks later. About sixty saboteurs arrived to try to disrupt the shooting, and one girl picked up a grouse which had been wounded in the wing. She told me she was going to take it to the vet in Skipton. It just so happened that I bumped into him a couple of days later and asked him if by any chance a girl had arrived with a grouse under her arm. 'Oh yes,' he said. 'She did come to the surgery.' I asked him how he had dealt with the situation. He told me that he had taken the bird into the operating theatre, where he had despatched it. He allowed a few minutes to pass, and then went back to the girl, to tell her he was sorry, but the grouse had passed away during the operation. 'My wife and I ate it for dinner last night, and it was delicious,' he confided.

Saboteurs arrived several times over the years, in half a dozen or so rickety vans, with the sole intention of causing mayhem and starting a fight. They always had a lawyer and a man with a camcorder with them. One week we were told that on the neighbouring moor, Dallowgill, one of these fellows had peed on the wife of a member of the shooting party while she sat in the bottom of a butt. I was standing with a charming American, Ned Cook, when word came over the radio that we were about to be hit by a bunch of particularly unpleasant saboteurs. Ned was six foot six inches tall, and had had a very distinguished war as a fighter pilot in the British Air Force. He was afraid of nothing. Nonetheless, I did tell him that if one of these thugs appeared he was to unload his guns and not to engage in conversation. At that moment a large man with an iron bar appeared on the top of our sunken butt, with the sun behind him, and looking extremely menacing. Before I had time to do anything, I saw Ned put the end of the barrels of his gun underneath the man's testicles. Ned looked up at him and said in his American drawl, 'Young man, I am told that I am not to talk to you. However, I *am* going to tell you one thing – if you piss on me or my friend here, you'll have no pecker.' The youth fled.

It was at another weekend party that I found myself sitting next to a charming Austrian girl called Svea Balfour. She told me that when she was eighteen she was despatched to England for a country house weekend, and her mother was paranoid about her losing her virginity during the weekend. 'Do anything you can think of to keep the young Englishmen at bay,' were her instructions. 'They are mostly wild, and very oversexed.' Svea told me that on arrival she found there were only two girls but five men in the party, and she realised that her mother had a point. Accordingly, she went upstairs and died her bush green. Before putting on her long dress she ran a transfer across her tummy (in case anyone should get that far) saying 'Please keep off the grass'. They went to the dance, and the night would have passed off without anyone finding out her secret, except for the fact that around midnight Svea was smitten with acute appendicitis. The next morning she woke up in hospital, having had a successful operation. She told me that she peered down to see what the wound looked like, and was amazed to find written across her tummy by the doctor 'Very sorry, I had to mow the lawn'.

In the spring of 1984 I took a house on the tennis ranch of Harry Hopman, at Bardmoor, Florida. Lucinda and I set off with the four Marchessini girls, my son Alexander, and four of my ten godchildren. There were seventy tennis courts, and we went everywhere by bicycle. It was a fantastic holiday. We came home fit and brown, and most of the children's tennis had come on enormously.

Alexander was already playing good tennis for his age and his most favourite opponent was my mother. Although she was in her late seventies, she still played a steady game and she taught her grandson well. She had been an excellent player in her youth and indeed, competed at Wimbledon. I was lying in my bath one evening, when a little head poked over the side. 'Hello Alexander' I said 'You made me jump. Is everything all right?'

'I'm afraid grandma's dead,' said Alexander.

'Heavens! Where is she?'

'On the tennis court.'

I flew out of the bath and raced up the garden. There was my mum, prostrate on the ground. As I went over, she began to stir. Alexander had sent up a lob and my mother had tripped while running backwards and smacked the back of her head on the asphalt, knocking herself out cold. She made a complete recovery, but hung up her racket from that day.

I had a good leg-pull with Charles Churchill at Christmas. He had mumbled to me and others that he was irritated by his brother Sunny asking me to Blenheim more often than he himself was invited. When the Heythrop Hounds met in front of the Palace in February I asked Anthony Adams, the huntsman, if he and the two Whippers-in would mind riding off to one side for a couple of minutes. Away they went, and I rode in behind the hounds on my horse *Archie* in my red swallow-tail coat, with the Palace behind me, and the hounds in front of me, I asked my girl-groom to take a photograph. Nine months later I had this picture made into a Christmas card – with a limited edition of *one* copy – which I sent off to Charles. He was furious, and telephoned his brother to say that Nick Peto had really over-cooked it this time: had Sunny seen the card I had sent everyone this year?

I was telephoned one day by a friend who had been told that I had behaved incredibly badly at lunch in the City the previous week. I asked him to tell me what he had heard and he said that I had been lunching with a pal in a corner table at Simpsons in the Strand. When we were three-quarters of the way through a very happy and merry lunch, a Nigerian, beautifully turned out, arrived at the adjacent table with two immaculate white men. The Nigerian ordered oxtail, and made a frightful fist of eating it. The knuckles flew all over the tablecloth, and it was with difficulty that he gathered them together back on to his plate. Apparently as I left to pay my bill I tapped the fellow on the shoulder, and pointing at the bones said to him, 'Anyone we know?' The man who rang to tell me this tale said that the other two gentlemen were senior Foreign Office dignitaries and the guest was the head of the Nigerian State Oil Company. I don't believe I did say any such thing, but being amused by the story, I decided not to deny it.

In that same spring of 1984, Candida Lycett Green's father, Sir John Betjeman, died. He was buried at St Enodoc Church, near Trebetherick in Cornwall. The funeral took place in appalling weather – driving rain, and a howling gale coming straight off the sea. We had to walk three quarters of a mile across the fields and the golf course, but my goodness, the journey and the wetting were worth it. The tiny church, with its low twisted spire, was incredibly dark inside, lit only by candles and two or three oil lamps. It was a beautiful service, made all the more dramatic by the tremendous storm outside. Sir John's coffin was carried back over the fields to a grave beside the lych-gate. It was a truly romantic send off. Later there was a full-blown memorial service in Westminster Abbey. Lady Chetwode had famously remarked to her daughter, when told she was to become engaged to JB: 'We invite people like that to tea, but we don't marry them.' She couldn't have been more wrong. The fun and laughter John Betjeman engendered in his lifetime, and the enormous pleasure his poems still give twenty years later, are legendary. It was a privilege to have known him.

CHAPTER 17

TATIANA

SEPTEMBER 2ND 1985 is a day I shall never forget as long as I live. I was staying in Angus for a week's fishing and shooting with Henry Keswick at Hunthill. It had rained hard all the previous day, and as a result I had decided to get up early to try and catch a salmon in the little spate river which ran down the valley below the lodge. Accordingly, I made my way down to the most likely pool with my trout rod at about seven in the morning. Hardly had I begun to fish, when I heard a shrill voice in the distance shouting 'Daddy, Daddy, Daddy.' I looked round to see Alexander, now twelve years old, running through the little grass enclosures in his pyjamas, with his dressing gown billowing out behind him. I couldn't imagine what had happened, but of course I put the rod down and ran to meet him. Exhausted, and completely out of breath Alexander said 'You must come back to the Lodge immediately. Lucinda is on the telephone; she says something dreadful has happened.'

I ran the mile or so as fast as I could, and went to the small glass telephone box in the hall. Lucinda told me that Tatiana, her youngest, had been in a terrible car accident in Athens. I told her I would come south as soon as I could get my things

157

together, and we would make plans when we knew what the doctors' prognosis was. Alexander and I packed up our clothes and guns, had a quick breakfast, and headed for home, five hundred miles away.

Tatiana was flown to England that day in a hospital plane, and admitted to the Wellington Humana Hospital in North West London. She was in a coma, and remained so for six months. Lucinda's world, and to a lesser extent mine, had collapsed around her ears. She thought everything of Tatiana, who seemed to have a glittering life ahead of her. She had done brilliantly at Wycombe Abbey School, and had been accepted for Oxford University; she played tennis for the Junior Oxfordshire Team, and was a stunningly attractive girl. The circumstances surrounding her accident were particularly tragic. Tatiana had checked in to fly home, only to be told by the airline that they were overbooked, and asked if she would mind returning the next morning – at which point they would fly her back Club Class. Being a student, and in no particular hurry, Tatty did not kick up a fuss, but instead, rang up a friend and arranged to go out to dinner. The young man with two of his male friends got drunk and the convertible Volkswagen Golf in which they were driving after dinner, hit the corner of a stationary lorry. The three boys escaped without a scratch, but Tatty lost part of the side of her head. She was left permanently injured, although her brain power is still one hundred per cent, and she never seems to have a 'down' day. Indeed, she is a lesson to us all with her cheerful and positive outlook. She lives with her mother, who has dedicated much of her life to her, and is to be wholly admired for her incredible unselfishness and love. But Tatty receives round the clock nursing care since she is unable to walk without help. She cannot speak.

CHAPTER 18

STILL FRIENDS

WITH THE BENEFIT of hindsight, Lucinda and I should never have married. We were, and still are, the best of friends, and there are things we love doing together, like playing golf. But, for various reasons, the marriage was never going to work – not least because the stings of conscience over my behaviour to Anne nearly crushed me. I suppose also, that Tatiana's accident was a contributing factor. However, we did stay together during this appalling and difficult time, with Lucinda almost full-time at Tatiana's bedside, and me trying to run things at Dean.

Two of our neighbours in the Cotswolds were the Mackinnons who lived over at Swinbrook. John was a delightful man, but with a very individualistic accent, rather plummy and slow. It was on the 4th January 1988 that I had an interesting rail journey with him from Charlbury to London. I was on my way to see the doctor, as I suspected I had a gall stone. There had been a long Christmas break, and on this Monday morning the train was likely to be very crowded. Just before I boarded, I noticed a small sign on each of the first class compartments saying that because of the extended holiday they were available also to second class passengers. This was good news indeed, and I made my way into a corner seat. There were three places on both sides of the compartment, and in the middle seats were a couple of railwaymen who had also spotted the sign on the window. They had their green and red flags under their arms, and wore leather British Rail caps. Just before the train was due to pull out I saw the unmistakable figure of John Mackinnon advancing down the platform, dark blue pin stripe suit, white shirt, Financial Times under one arm and a briefcase and umbrella. I thought to myself, 'John, I love you very much, but on this occasion I do hope you don't get into this compartment.' The next thing I knew the door slid back, and a large red face peered in. 'Morning Nick,' he said, sitting himself down diagonally away from me in the corner by the door. The train pulled out, and I was about to go back to my newspaper when John boomed out 'I hear you've buggered your back? So have I. I've got three hunters, all cost over £4,000, and they're eating their heads off in the stables.' The two railwaymen looked bemused. As we shunted slowly through Hanborough, John exploded once again. 'Have you been shooting with Sunny yet this year?'

'No,' I murmured.

'Well I have, and you see that wood over there? Why on earth does he always do it this way?'

At this point he demonstrated with his arms flying all over his end of the carriage.

'The birds would fly so much better if he did it that way.'

Again flailing of arms. The railwaymen looked very surprised. After this, I pretended to fall asleep, but as we entered Paddington station there was another explosion.

'My God,' said John, 'I think White's is still shut!'

161

By this stage he was including the railwaymen in his conversation, and seemed to address his next question as much to them as to me.

'Where do you think a fellow can get a good dinner tonight, if that is the case?'

I think that if the two men got into the train as socialists, they must have got out as communists.

I went off to see my doctor, who gave me some medicine, which he told me should help me 'pass' the stone. When I arrived back at the station in the afternoon I desperately wanted to spend a penny, so I disappeared into the Gentlemens adjacent to Platform 1, along with about fifty other people. I opened my fly buttons and found myself in the most excruciating pain. I let out a tremendous cry as I bent over the urinal. All the other men, in whatever state of undress, disappeared up the exit steps as fast as they could, in order to distance themselves from this screaming lunatic. My stone was 'passed', and so I went to the telephone to give the glad tidings to my doctor.

'Did you manage to keep the stone, as I told you?'

'No,' I said, 'it was neither the time nor the place to go digging around for a tiny crystal.'

All in all, it had been quite a day.

Towards the end of the eighties I went skiing to both Klosters and Val d'Isère. As I mentioned earlier, skiing was not my forte. During the week in Klosters I had two or three disasters. At one stage, my guide, Mia and I went to the very top of the mountain. 'Mia,' I said, 'it was easy enough to get me up here, but it is you who are responsible for getting me down.' Mia was the World Champion Hot-Dogger, a ski sport in which one turns somersaults and generally performs crazy acrobatic jumps over ramps and moguls. She was immensely powerful, and seemed to have every confidence that we would negotiate the various runs back to the village without problems. The first thing that happened, soon after we got off the button lift, was that Mia traversed over the parallel ruts that everyone was making with their skis as they went up the mountain on the lift. This was easy enough for her, as she simply did a little jump over these deep divots in the snow. When it came to my turn, I funked the little jump and my skis locked in to the tram lines. I found myself hurtling down the hill unable to go to right or left. On the next upcoming button was a ski guide, covered with bright orange anti-sun cream on his lips, his cheek bones and his nose. He wore an orange bandana, and was smiling at me. I believe he imagined I was a good skier and was about to leap out of the way at the last minute. Just before the moment of impact, his look changed to one of horror, as he realised that some idiot was going to knock him off his button. Sure enough, I crashed into him and we both went sprawling into the snow. The poor man had a class of about twenty behind him, and as each one passed they roared with laughter. He wasn't pleased, because he had to ski right down to the bottom of the hill to catch an empty button again. I was, in due course, stood upright by Mia, and dusted down. She also thought the episode hysterically funny, but I reckon I was lucky not to have hurt myself badly.

One of those in our party was Libby Beckett. It was at her fortieth birthday party a year or two earlier that I had upset her rather left-wing mother-in-law. A most lavish dance had been given for Libby at Rievaulx Abbey in Yorkshire. I had a wonderful evening, and as dawn broke I knew no pain. I tottered into the garden to spend a penny, and was in full swing when Libby's mother-in-law came round the corner and stood before me, both amazed and disgusted.

I said, 'Hello Pinky – meet Perky.'

'You are quite revolting,' she said, and turned on her heel.

Libby and I were about the same standard on the slopes, and some mornings we were sent off together with a German guide, who spoke poor English. After a particularly heavy night I ventured out of the hotel onto the slippery pavement. I was a little late, and our German was waiting. There was no sign of Libby.

'Velly sleepy,' opened the German.

'I've had a late night,' I replied grumpily, 'but I am not sleepy.'

'No' he said raising his voice, 'velly sleepy.'

I tried again. 'I can see it is very slippy, but thank you.'

At which point the guide raised his voice even louder and shouted. 'No!! – velly sleepy?' It was only then that I grasped what he was saying – where is Libby? Ever since that day poor Libby has gained a nickname from me, and she is always known as 'Velly Sleepy'.

Towards the end of that week the lower slopes had become sheet ice; it was very cold indeed, and had not snowed for three weeks. There was only one route back into the village, which was steep and with sharp bends – which did not suit my skiing at all. There were literally hundreds of people whizzing past me, as I approached a near verticle harpin, and I told Mia that there was no way I was going to get round the corner. 'Don't worry,' she said, 'I will go in front of you, and I will stand on the corner at the edge of the cliff. Point your skis directly at me, and run into me – you will be fine. I promise to hold you.' When she was in position I set off as slowly as I could down the hill (snow plough position), but as I was travelling on ice I seemed to have no control of my skis, and I felt myself rapidly gathering speed. Mia stood her ground bravely. When I was two thirds of the way down the slope towards her, it seemed like I was going a hundred miles an hour. Mia was still in position. Just before I ran into her, she took two quick steps to the right, and I sailed over the precipice. In fact, I landed in the top of a fir tree which was only a couple of metres from where Mia stood. I clung on to this waving pine, as if I was a koala bear. I was completely covered in snow, and one of my skis had come undone at the moment I hit the tree, and was never seen again. The conundrum then was how to get me back on the ski slope. Although as the crow (or I) flew it was only two metres, there was no way I could take such a direct route back.

By this stage there were fifty or sixty hysterical skiers standing next to Mia, laughing till their ski suits burst. I actually had to slither the whole way down the tree, into deep snow at its base. Luckily, the snow was hard enough to hold my weight, or I doubt whether I would be telling this tale now. One of the guides who, by this stage, had arrived above me threw down a red rope with a noose on it, and I put this under my shoulders. I was then unceremoniously hauled up the twenty feet or so to rejoin Mia. I asked her why on earth she had side-stepped, to which she replied that I was going so fast that I would have taken her over the cliff as well, and she would rather I went on my own.

My nightmare did not end there, because of course I only had one ski. Mia struck a deal, and said she would ski down to the village with me on her shoulders, provided I took her to the night club later that evening. It was already practically dark, and almost everyone else had gone on down; all I could think about was having a large drink to settle my jangliing nerves. I agreed to her proposal, and clambered onto her back. This too was a terrifying experience. Mia skied so fast and so surely with me perched above her, but I felt at any moment we would disappear over yet another precipice. When we got back to the hotel, word had gone before us as to what had happened. The drinks were ready, and so was a hot bath. I did take Mia to the night club, but I am afraid I must have been a great disappointment to her, so exhausted was I.

In October 1988 I went on a fantastic yacht called *Albacorra*, jointly owned by two friends, Christopher Heath and Oliver Baring. There were six men and three women in the party. As we cruised past one of the Greek islands I told my hosts that I knew a beautiful girl who lived there and suggested that I go ashore and ask her to come on board for dinner that night.

The *Albacorra* dropped anchor, and I set off. I had with me in the tender a beautician from Manchester called Jenny who was one of our crew, and I had already discussed my plans with her. Having arrived at the little harbour, Jenny and I repaired to the nearest bar. There she proceeded to make me up in drag. She had brought a minute ra-ra skirt for me, a tight T-shirt, a wig – the works.

We made our way back to the yacht, arriving alongside at 8.30, in good time for dinner. Nic and Suki Paravicini were on board, and he was in a high state of excitement at the prospect of the arrival of a new lady. As I clambered (ladylike) up the ladder, and poked my head over the deck, a large hand appeared. 'Well, hello. I'm Nic Paravicini, do let me help you aboard.' I have to admit, no one was taken in for long, but Oliver did put me on his right at dinner.

Around this time, my old friend Chips Keswick told me that he was very worried about his middle son, Toby, who had just turned twenty two. He sported a long pigtail, and showed no inclination either to go to University or to get a job. Chips was Chairman of Hambro's Bank, and he asked his son to lunch. Toby arrived, the top half looking very respectable – shirt, tie, jacket. The bottom half was a bit disappointing since he was wearing jeans and trainers.

Undaunted, they set off in the lift for the top floor, where there was a very grand dining room – panelled walls, chande-liers, a butler, excellent claret. Chips never took more than an hour off for lunch, and the coffee arrived at ten to two. He bit the bullet and said to Toby, 'The reason I have asked you to lunch is to try and find out what you are going to do with yourself. Are you going to look for employment? What are your plans?' Toby's eyes moved slowly around the vast room, and after a minute or so they settled on his father.

'Well, Dad,' said Toby, 'you seem to be doing OK. Why don't you kick on for both of us?'

The late eighties were marred by several disasters, and so

my switchback life continued. I had joined Lloyds as a 'name' and found myself on the dreaded Feltrim Syndicate 540. This was to relieve me of all my money over the next few years. I seemed to spend more time with my bank manager than anywhere else. I never found the opportunity to use Charles Egerton's repost. When he was in his early twenties his bank manager said to him, 'Mr Egerton, the amount of your overdraft is more than I earn in a whole year. What have you got to say to that?'

'Well,' said Charles, 'all I can say is that you must be in the wrong job.'

Lucinda and I were asked for a weekend's shooting with Peter and 'Milla Halifax at Garrowby. The Queen and Prince Philip were also staying, so the weekend was memorable – but, as it turned out, for the wrong reasons. After a long discussion during one of the pheasant drives Lucinda and I agreed that we should separate. We were friends, but we both felt we would do better on our own.

That same month my favourite golden retriever, Kelpie, had to be put down, as did *Willy* my much loved hunter. Lucinda and I went to see a local solicitor to discuss our divorce. I told him that there were no children, and no money was going to change hands either. 'How much would you charge to represent both of us, and write two letters to the Oxford County Court?' I asked. He said that it was unheard of for one solicitor to represent both parties, but I managed to persuade him. 'Would £500 be all right?' he said.

'For two letters, I'll give you £150,' I replied, producing three fifties from my pocket.

'OK, it's a deal.' he said. Not many divorces come cheaper than that.

At the same time as all this was going on, Dean Manor was sold, which brings this memoir to a natural conclusion.

By way of an epilogue, I must add that on December 19th 1991 I remarried. Zoë and I had known each other for many years. I love her beyond measure. When she enters a room her radiant smile brightens everything, and everyone. Rupert Lycett Green – who has attended all three of my weddings – was my witness, while Camilla Parker Bowles, one of our oldest friends, did the honours for Zoë. At the lunch afterwards, in a little restaurant behind the Chelsea Town Hall, the small gathering included Annie (my first wife) and her husband Martin Summers, who had donned a chauffeur's uniform and drove us the hundred yards in 'The Major' – his 1961 Armstrong Siddeley.

So life has taken an upswing once again. Zoë and I live in a pretty Cotswold cottage, with a lovely garden, and three dogs. We see a lot of my son Alexander, of whom I am enormously proud and he has recently married a delightful girl, Samantha. I am in good health.

I am a very lucky fellow indeed.

On his deathbed W.C. Fields uncharacteristically asked for a man of God to visit him. When the priest arrived, he was surprised to see the dying man sitting up in bed, leafing through the Bible. 'What are you looking for?' he inquired. 'Loopholes,' murmured Fields. I already know how he felt.

I owe a big thank you to Wendy Turner, who worked so hard at typing out my tapes. However, each time I went to see her in Chipping Norton, Wendy would hand me the sheets of paper, and tell me how much I owed, but never was there any comment on the contents.

When I was about to collect the last chapter, I said to Zoë, 'Come with me to Wendy's. I am determined to get a reaction out of her on my last visit.' As usual, Wendy handed me the typing and the tape, and said 'That will be £20 please.' So I said, 'It's a load of rubbish really, isn't it?'

'Well, I think so,' replied Wendy earnestly.

WHO'S WHO